"*Survivor. Overcomer. Counselor. Speaker. Enc*[...] Lisa Saruga. You will be gripped by her hone[...] chapters of this book. More than that, you wi[...] mode to wholeness. If you or someone you know has experienced trauma, this is one of the most important books you can read. Every church and Christian counseling organization should place *The Trauma Tree* in the hands of those who need to know it's possible to move from surviving to thriving."

—Carol Kent, founder and executive director of Speak Up Ministries,
speaker, and author of *When I Lay My Isaac Down*

"*The Trauma Tree* is a hope-filled book that will help any reader identify the right role of trauma in his or her life or the life of someone they love. The strengths-based, biblical approach Lisa shares as a therapist and someone with personal experience provides the right balance of authentic empathy and practical tools for education and healing. I highly recommend *The Trauma Tree* and will use it with clients or friends to help them understand the role of trauma and adverse experiences in the lives of the ones they love."

—Brenda L. Yoder, LMHC, therapist, school counselor,
and author of *Uncomplicated*

"Healing from trauma is some of the sweetest revenge after you've endured the unthinkable. Who better to plant the seeds, water the flowers, and help hand you the beautiful bouquet that is forged through life's desert experiences than a trauma counselor who has healed from her own unimaginable trauma and lived to write about it? We all bear the scars of the pain from our past, but what the Enemy intended for harm, God will use for good if we allow. Lisa Saruga is proof of that. May her story and her professional experience encourage you on your healing journey."

—Dr. Michelle Bengtson, clinical neuropsychologist, award-winning
author of *The Hem of His Garment* and *Sacred Scars*,
and host of *Your Hope-Filled Perspective*

"The combination of her lived experience and her years as a professional therapist make Lisa Saruga a most trustworthy guide for those walking the healing journey from trauma to wellness. Thoughtful, informative, and compassionate, this book is a much-needed gift."

—Steve Siler, founder and director of Music for the Soul

"Lisa Saruga delivers a compelling story about her decades-long quest for justice and healing. Her remarkable personal courage in dealing with not only trauma but a system that all too often fails to protect victims and survivors is a testament to the strength of her faith."

—Brian Ross, correspondent on the Law & Crime Network and author of *The Madoff Chronicles*

The Trauma Tree

GOING BEYOND SURVIVAL, GROWING TOWARD WHOLENESS

Lisa Saruga

FOREWORD BY ANGELINE BOULLEY
#1 *New York Times* best-selling author of *Firekeeper's Daughter*

KREGEL
PUBLICATIONS

Published by Kregel Publications, a division of Kregel Inc., 2450 Oak Industrial Dr. NE, Grand Rapids, MI 49505. www.kregel.com.

Published in association with Books & Such Literary Management, www.booksandsuch.com.

The persons and events portrayed in this book have been used with permission. To protect the privacy of these individuals, some names and identifying details have been changed.

This book is not intended as a substitute for professional medical or psychological services. This book is not meant to be used, nor should it be used, to diagnose or treat any medical or psychological condition. Readers are advised to consult their own medical advisers whose responsibility it is to determine the condition of, and best treatment for, the reader.

All Scripture quotations, unless otherwise indicated, are taken from the Holy Bible, New International Version®, NIV®. Copyright © 1973, 1978, 1984, 2011 by Biblica, Inc.™ Used by permission of Zondervan. All rights reserved worldwide. www.zondervan.com. The "NIV" and "New International Version" are trademarks registered in the United States Patent and Trademark Office by Biblica, Inc.™

Scripture quotations marked ESV are from the ESV® Bible (The Holy Bible, English Standard Version®), copyright © 2001 by Crossway, a publishing ministry of Good News Publishers. Used by permission. All rights reserved. The ESV text may not be quoted in any publication made available to the public by a Creative Commons license. The ESV may not be translated in whole or in part into any other language.

Scripture quotations marked KJV are from the King James Version.

Scripture quotations marked MSG are taken from *The Message*, copyright © 1993, 2002, 2018 by Eugene H. Peterson. Used by permission of NavPress. All rights reserved. Represented by Tyndale House Publishers.

Scripture quotations marked NLT are taken from the *Holy Bible*, New Living Translation, copyright ©1996, 2004, 2015 by Tyndale House Foundation. Used by permission of Tyndale House Publishers, Carol Stream, Illinois 60188. All rights reserved.

Scripture quotations marked NLV are taken from the New Life Version copyright © 1969 and 2003. Used by permission of Barbour Publishing, Inc., Uhrichsville, Ohio, 44683. All rights reserved.

Italics in Scripture indicate the author's added emphasis.

Cataloging-in-Publication Data is available from the Library of Congress.

ISBN 978-0-8254-4874-4, print
ISBN 978-0-8254-7422-4, epub
ISBN 978-0-8254-7421-7, Kindle

Printed in the United States of America
25 26 27 28 29 30 31 32 33 34 / 5 4 3 2 1

To those who wonder if joy can be found this side of heaven.

Spoiler alert: It can.

Contents

CONTENTS

Foreword

Trauma is universal; healing is uniquely individual. How we find solid footing atop the rubble of violence and loss is neither prescriptive nor predictable.

I met Lisa Saruga when we worked in the same residence hall during our junior and senior years of college. Our connection was instant and, spoiler alert, is going strong thirty-something years later. As our friendship blossomed, we shared stories about our upbringing. We both grew up with larger-than-life fathers whose approval or judgment defined our childhoods. We shared a similar religious upbringing, each conflating our father with Our Father—an all-knowing, powerful figure we loved and feared. Our college years were supposed to be about gaining independence, forming our own ideas, developing our intellects, and caring for our physical, emotional, and spiritual selves.

At one point, my friend disclosed that something horrible happened to her during our freshman year. Without another word, I somehow knew she was the girl who had been violently attacked in her dorm room. The girl whose assault was reported in the student newspaper. That brutal crime changed how I felt about the safety of small-town college life and was one of my earliest experiences of questioning my faith. If God was almighty, then where was He that night for the girl in the dorm?

Decades later, both Lisa and I were writing manuscripts—her, a memoir about the aftermath of that night, and me, a young-adult mystery set within my Ojibwe community. We entered the querying trenches around the same time. We commiserated over rejections and celebrated each step forward.

In *Firekeeper's Daughter,* eighteen-year-old Daunis Fontaine witnesses the murder of a loved one and is reluctantly thrust into an undercover drug investigation within her Ojibwe community. Telling a realistic coming-of-age story set on an Indian reservation meant including unpleasant truths faced by too many Native women and girls, and in particular, sexual violence.

A 2010 National Institute of Justice study found that 84 percent of Native American (American Indian and Alaska Native) women have experienced violence in their lifetimes.[1] This translates to more than four in five Native women. More than half (56.1 percent) have experienced sexual violence in their lifetimes. More than one in three (39.8 percent) had experienced violence within the past year.

In the story, Daunis is raped by a non-Native man who knows that, because his crime takes place on tribal land and his victim is Native, the federal government rather than the tribe or state has criminal jurisdiction. The emboldened perpetrator knows the lack of federal resources means it is unlikely he'll ever be charged, prosecuted, and convicted of his crime. Though Daunis is denied legal justice, she finds healing through different methods.

In *The Trauma Tree: Going Beyond Survival, Growing Toward Wholeness,* Lisa Saruga offers the visual of a pear tree to illustrate her approach to healing trauma. It is a method I can easily imagine Daunis using as part of her healing. Lisa's personal experience with trauma and her decades as a licensed therapist have given her a totally unique perspective on the journey through trauma. This book will show you how to do more than simply survive your trauma; it will guide you into living a life of abundant joy and peace. I would like to see a book like this made available in my community and other Native communities. It is a resource that speaks to the heart without placing people in distress.

Miigwech (thank you), dearest Lisa.

ANGELINE BOULLEY

Author of the *New York Times* best sellers *Firekeeper's Daughter* and *Warrior Girl Unearthed*

Introduction

It is likely that you have acquired this book because you or someone you love has endured a traumatic event or is enduring ongoing trauma in life. Let me begin by saying, I am so sorry for your experience. Following trauma, we often feel a mix of emotions, not the least of which is hopelessness. What has been done cannot be undone, and it is difficult to see how the pain will ever end.

Friend, I get it. I understand your pain not only through the eyes of a trauma therapist but because I, too, have survived major trauma. I have first-person understanding of the devastating, crushing confusion and pain that ride in on trauma's coattails.

Big "T" Trauma entered my life in the form of a violent crime when I was eighteen years old. Shortly after starting college, I was sleeping in my dorm room alone. I awoke in the early morning hours to find a man wearing a ski mask crouched beside my bed. By the time he left my room, I had been knifed, nearly suffocated, and violated in unspeakable ways. I never saw my attacker's face. Although I was taken to the hospital for treatment and evidence collection, my case was closed after a few months for lack of leads.

I know the pain of trauma. I understand how overwhelming and ugly and brutal the aftermath is. When big "T" Trauma occurs, we often see our lives as having been divided into two parts: before and after. I resisted this division. Following this event, I was determined to move forward. I had been a happy college student the day before the attack and was determined to continue as such after. My plan was to not look back. I avoided talking to anyone about the experience—not my family, not my friends, and certainly not a counselor. I wanted to just get over it.

The problem with trauma is that we never simply get *over* it. The truth is, we have to walk *through* it. The pain is inescapable, even if we choose to ignore the trauma. I successfully ignored mine for thirty-five years. Ironically, during those years I became a licensed professional counselor and walked with many others *through* the process of healing. I truly believed I had gotten *over* my own trauma.

It became clear that I was wrong when, after thirty-five years, the identity of the man who attacked me was exposed and my cold case reopened. The unprocessed pain and fear surfaced in ways I never could have predicted. This would lead to my own battle with post-traumatic stress disorder (PTSD). I thought I had a clear understanding of PTSD and the journey to healing. I was, after all, a seasoned trauma therapist. I now believe that no one is an "expert" in trauma until they have walked that road of healing themselves.

Following my attack, I struggled with some of the words that were thrown around. People referred to me as a *survivor*. While I knew this was meant to encourage me, I often felt like an impostor. If the definition of a survivor is one who hasn't stopped breathing, then yes, I survived. Yet I knew people meant more—meant strength—when using this term. And I didn't feel like I deserved the label of strength.

I was also confused by the term *victim*. People would say, "You don't want to be a victim." But I was, wasn't I? According to the Oxford Advanced Learner's Dictionary, the definition of the word *victim* is "a person who has been attacked, injured or killed as the result of a crime, a disease, an accident, etc."[1] That means everyone who has experienced trauma has been a victim, yet it is frowned upon to acknowledge this. Why does this word carry such a stigma?

A woman who was grieving the loss of her daughter shared with me that her daughter had been called a *survivor* after being sexually assaulted. This mom was angry in her grief. She poured out the reality that her daughter turned to drinking to cover her pain. Her daughter's marriage failed. She lost her career. And alcohol's firm grip on her eventually led to her dying from liver failure.

No wonder this mother—and others like her—would rebel against the word *survivor*.

After talking with this mother, I was inspired to write a poem. I am guessing some readers may identify with these words.

Am I a Survivor?

You call me a survivor, but have I survived?
I mean—I AM still alive,
But the hole in my soul is a really dark pit.
I'm not sure how long I can handle it.
I've been called "brave," even told I'm a hero,
But I screamed like a baby whose belly's on zero.
To be called a survivor is meant to empower me,
But the victim inside is trying to devour me.
I need to be heard, believed, and supported.
This victim needs justice now that I've reported.
No face, no case. No case, no victim.
No victim? No worries—no need to convict him.
Truth is, this is not a victimless crime.
I don't feel like a survivor most of the time.

So I drink to silence the victim inside,
Play the role of survivor who hasn't yet died.
But the pain can only be silenced for so long,
And when pain meets shame, it's all just so wrong.
I can't find any other way to escape.
Can you blame me for wanting to self-medicate?
Drink some more—more regret.
Stuck in Depression's heavy net.
Paste a smile—play the part,
But you can't see what's dead in my heart.
Survivor? How long can I pretend it
Before I just choose to end it?
But what kind of survivor would I be
If I let *this* be the end of me?
Stand tall—play the victor,
Then drink more liquor.
My next sip may end my strife,
Maybe even take my life
. . . Would I still be a survivor?

Although my own trauma arrived dressed in a ski mask, I will talk about many forms of trauma in this book. The effects of trauma on our brains are similar regardless of what type of trauma we experience. We will look at two categories of trauma: big "T" Trauma and little "t" trauma. Neither are to be confused with drama, which we all experience from time to time.

Big "T" Traumas are deeply disturbing, often life-threatening events. Common examples of big "T" Trauma are natural disasters, sexual violence, proximity to a violent death, or serious car accidents. Big "T" Trauma, or even witnessing big "T" events, can lead to PTSD. First responders and people who have been in military combat zones are examples of witnesses who may experience post-trauma symptoms.

Little "t" traumas are highly distressing events that don't fall into the category of big "T" Trauma. Non-life-threatening injuries, emotional abuse, bullying, and loss of significant relationships are examples of little "t" trauma. Current diagnostic criteria states that PTSD can only be diagnosed in those who have experienced or witnessed big "T" Trauma, but this is unfortunate. Chronic little "t" trauma can be as emotionally damaging as a single big "T" event. The symptoms can be very similar. Anytime I use the word *trauma*, know that it can apply to either type of trauma.

The diagnosis of PTSD will come up frequently in this book. PTSD is a group of symptoms that commonly occur following big "T" Trauma and chronic little "t" trauma; however, I will also share a more optimistic and realistic view of these symptoms than I feel current language surrounding PTSD provides. I hope to reframe everything you might think you know about PTSD.

When my cold case was reopened, I wondered why God would allow the pain to return. Why did the symptoms of trauma plague me after so many years? Why couldn't He have left well enough alone? I was perfectly fine pretending the trauma had never occurred. As I questioned God, a Scripture verse repeatedly came to my attention. I wrote the words down.

> I remain confident of this:
> I will see the goodness of the LORD
> in the land of the living.
> (Psalm 27:13)

I had prayed that I would see justice in this lifetime—that my perpetrator would be held accountable in a court of law, not just at the final judgment. For a long time after the cold case was reopened, I felt this Scripture was promising me legal justice. I was wrong. My perpetrator would never be charged with this crime.

While that may sound like defeat, I have good news! Although it may seem that trauma has stolen all hope for your future and won't be healed unless you experience a happy ending, *trauma is a liar*. We may never see a happy ending to our trauma in this lifetime, but we can experience the goodness of the Lord again. Psalm 27 is a psalm of both lament and confidence. The two can coexist. Verse 13 reveals that God wants so much more for us than just survival. He hears our laments and offers us life beyond the trauma.

The goodness of the Lord is this: God will restore love, joy, peace, patience, kindness, goodness, faithfulness, gentleness, and self-control in abundance (Galatians 5:22–23; John 10:10). He will do so *in the land of the living*. My friend, there is life after trauma. I believe this book will reveal the very real healing that is available through the grace of Jesus. I believe your life ahead can, and should, include joy and peace.

May the Lord refresh your spirit as we walk through this journey together. May He support us as we lament what we will never get *over* and encourage us to be confident in His goodness as He carries us *through*.

The Parable of the Pear Tree

*L*ong after my personal big "T" Trauma incident that introduced me to the reality of genuine trauma and its long-lasting effects, I experienced a "drama" with a cherished pear tree.[1] I want to share that story with you as a parable we will refer to from time to time throughout the book.

I could hardly even look at Barry the day after it happened. My shiny new husband seemed much less . . . well, shiny.

Barry sat in a recliner watching TV and sipping his diet peach iced tea as if this were just any other day. He must have noticed my disgusted side-eye glance in his direction.

"I didn't mean it," he said.

"I tried to tell you this would happen." My tone was punctuated with disappointment, despair, and anger. The loss seemed unbearable. I was grieving, but he just seemed to carry on as if nothing had happened.

"From my perspective, it looked like everything was okay," he said.

"Your perspective was wrong! I told you exactly what was going to happen, but you didn't listen." The words came out like gale-force winds directed at his paper-thin excuses.

"Look," he said, "I really think it will be okay."

"'Okay?' I have nurtured and tended to that tree for *months*. When we got married and blended our families together, it represented our union. It is not 'okay' to just carry on and forget about it." My eyes were burning again, and I couldn't seem to swallow the lump in my throat.

"Oh, come on. Don't you think that might be a bit dramatic?" he asked.

I took a long, deep breath and then spoke very slowly, quietly. "Dramatic? Are you saying that her trauma was not significant enough to warrant even a small amount of regret or remorse on your part?"

"I know you are upset, sweetheart," he said with a chuckle, "but this is not the end of the world. We really are okay."

I couldn't believe my ears. "This was a gift that arrived at the exact right moment to represent our binding together as a family. I don't know if I can bear to start again, caring for and nurturing another tender toddler tree."

The object of devastation was a beautiful, perfect little pear tree that some friends had given Barry and me as a wedding gift. Because the tree was small and winters are hard in Michigan, I had raised her in our garage for nearly a year. I wrapped her pot in a blanket so she would be warm at night. I fed her nourishing, gentle plant food and gave her plenty of water. She was small enough that, on particularly cold nights, I could cover her branches with a single plastic garbage bag to keep the frost from her tender new limbs.

Pear trees represent life and longevity. Because my husband and I had each been married before, the New Bradford Pear was the perfect wedding gift for our newly blended family. In giving it to us, our friends were wishing us abundant life and longevity in our marriage. Still, I had been a bit concerned. "I don't want to seem ungrateful," I said to them, "but aren't Bradford Pear trees kind of a nuisance? I have heard they are weak and smell bad. Aren't they an invasive species?"

"Not to worry," our friends said. "This is a variety called a *New* Bradford Pear. Its trunk will grow straight and true, and its branches will be strong enough to weather your Michigan storms. It will have all the beauty of a Bradford Pear, but it will be fragrant and strong. This is what we wish for your marriage—that you will grow together, straight and true, focused on God above; that God will give you the strength to weather any storm; and that your love will give off a fragrance that is pleasing to the Lord and to all who know you."

How could we go wrong with that?

We would watch this tree grow as our marriage and family grew stronger and more rooted in love each day. Her flowers in the spring would remind us of the beauty of life and that, even after rough seasons, our family would blossom under God's tender care. Her beautiful foliage would be the last to fall in autumn, reminding us to be strong and resilient when harsh times lay ahead.

After caring for the tree in the garage, we planted her in the front yard. She was small, maybe six feet tall. Also in the front was a very tall pine tree I didn't particularly care for. It was too large for our yard, and grass wouldn't grow in its shade. Besides, it cast a shadow on the little pear tree, and the pear needed all the sunshine it could get. We decided together to cut the unwanted pine tree down.

As my husband began to saw a wedge shape out of the trunk of the massive pine, I noticed the cut was facing toward the little pear tree.

"Barry, I think we should adjust the angle of this cut. I know you want to avoid the telephone wires, but this is going to land on the pear tree."

From where Barry was standing, it looked like the pine would clear the pear tree just fine.

A formidable crack sounded from the large pine. "Timber!" Barry yelled.

We hurried to make sure we were out of the way and turned our backs to avoid any debris that would fly out of its wake. As if in slow motion, the great pine groaned and tipped, falling with a great whoosh into our small front yard. As we heard it settle on the ground, we slowly turned to see if it had missed the wires, our home . . .

And the pear tree.

The words "I told you so!" threatened to spill from my mouth. The large, heavy trunk of the pine had landed directly on top of our baby pear.

The pear now consisted of a straight, perfect trunk and two spindly, broken branches pitifully reaching in opposite directions. I assumed she would die, but even if she lived, she would never be the same.

Now she would serve as a reminder of the ugliness and destruction that occurs when a husband and wife can't communicate and can't find common ground. Was this what our marriage would look like? Would it be a weak, disfigured, hideous mess?

As our conversation the following day progressed, my husband remained calm and spoke with sensitivity. "Hon, I really think this tree will be okay. It will fill in with new branches. Things will be tough for a while, but it will still grow and flourish. This tree has had a great start, and it is strong. Let's have faith and continue to tend to the tree."

This little tree had suffered a big "T" Trauma. Its very life was threatened, and even if it survived, its future would look grim. Those of us who loved her had to give up our hopes and expectations for her future. Shattered dreams can be the most difficult part of trauma. Although the tree wasn't yet dead, the promise of a beautiful future had all but expired. What good is survival if hope has died?

PART I

Survival Mode

CHAPTER 1

Understanding Trauma

F ollowing my attack, I did what many people do after experiencing big "T" Trauma: I dissociated from the trauma as a survival response. Dissociation is a search for a sense of normality because the truth is too difficult to face. But this survival technique detaches a person from reality. If we do not process the reality of the trauma, its effects remain fully intact, stored silently in the brain until something triggers the stored memory.

Our first step in "going beyond survival" is to correctly name the things that keep us stuck in mere survival mode.

Trauma is a highly charged response to any distressing event that exceeds what we think of as a normal human experience. Trauma involves loss, pain, shock, and often, devastating alterations to future plans, expectations, and goals. As I mentioned in the introduction, trauma falls into two categories: big "T" Trauma and little "t" trauma. Both have a similar impact on us physically, emotionally, and spiritually.

Memories associated with strong emotions are stored in a little part of our brain called the *amygdala*. It isn't a part of our brain that we access consciously. Our strong emotional memories hide in the amygdala until something reminds this part of our brain of the past trauma. When this happens, the amygdala dumps the stored emotions into our system, along with adrenaline and other chemicals and hormones that attend those emotions. This is what we call *triggering*. It can result in flashbacks, nightmares, sudden emotional changes, hypervigilance, and more.

NO ONE IS IMMUNE

I avoided processing my trauma for more than three decades before I was triggered and my amygdala unleashed the full emotional impact of my trauma. By then I had been working with other trauma survivors for many years and had seen the effects of PTSD every day with my clients. As I said, I thought my understanding of trauma made me immune to ever experiencing it myself . . .

Until the day I received a phone call from a detective at my alma mater.

In an instant, I experienced a flood of emotions I recognized from thirty-five years earlier. It was like I was eighteen years old again. Terror flooded my body. It was as if that box of memories I had stored on a shelf in my mind had been flung open, and the memories were scattered before me like well-preserved photographs. I relived every detail of that morning—what I had worn, the sound of my attacker's voice, even the smell in the room.

I began to have nightmares and night terrors and found it difficult to control my emotions. I cried easily, and I couldn't concentrate on small tasks. I learned quickly that I was not immune to PTSD. I had simply delayed the experience.

GRIEF IS UNPREDICTABLE

The pain and suffering that follow trauma can make survival feel like a life sentence. Elisabeth Kübler-Ross researched grief and gave us the first model for the stages of grief: denial, anger, bargaining, depression, and acceptance. We tend to think of the stages of grief in relation to the issue of death and dying, but these same stages are present when we suffer any significant loss. Trauma always involves loss of some kind, and loss inevitably leads to a season of grief. (More on this in chapter 2.)

From the conversation Barry and I had the day after the slaying of the pear tree, it's clear I had bounced from denial to anger. As for Barry, was he stuck in denial as he predicted the tree would live and thrive? Or was it hopeful optimism? Sometimes it's difficult to tell the difference.

> *Trauma always involves loss of some kind, and loss inevitably leads to a season of grief.*

The stages of grief are not clean, uniform, or orderly. We don't really progress from one stage to the next. Instead, we bounce around between the different stages like a steel ball in a pinball machine. One minute the world seems good and whole. We believe life will go on and our hopes and dreams will be fulfilled. The next minute we are angry and lashing out at anyone who crosses our path. Often we don't even know what we are angry about.

Each of us who has experienced trauma has a unique story. We often compare our story with others' in an effort to comfort ourselves. We tell ourselves our story is less significant than someone else's to minimize our trauma. Or, conversely, we believe our trauma is so much worse that no one can possibly understand.

I encourage you to embrace your story and your need for healing. Just as each person grieves differently, each path to healing will differ—but there is a path forward for every one of us.

I found a Christian forensic psychologist who worked with me for several months. Processing the long-ignored trauma was not easy. I also told my adult children and my husband about the attack. I allowed my family and friends to support me. And I asked God to reveal how my trauma could somehow be used for His purposes.

These steps taught me some helpful and some not-so-helpful things along the way. Perhaps most significantly, I learned that healing is possible, even when this world offers no happy ending.

WHEN THE BIBLE ISN'T HELPFUL

Don't most of us start life blissfully unaware that bad events could be lurking in our future? We live life with reckless abandon, excited for what the future might hold. Unfortunately, sooner or later, we all suffer trauma and loss. It often takes us by surprise, as though we thought we'd be the first human being to live a life uncomplicated by negative events.

Some people pull individual verses from the Bible and deduce that, if we do right by God, we will never experience bad things. For example, Proverbs 1:33 says, "Whoever listens to me will live in safety and be at ease, without fear of harm."

Let's not forget that Proverbs comes only two books after Job, where we learn that bad things *do* happen to good people. Job was a righteous and blameless man, yet he experienced the loss of his wealth, his children perishing in a natural disaster, severe physical illness, loss of reputation, the rejection of his friends, a lack of support from his wife, depression, and a whole host of other significant traumatic events. But how can the above proverb be true if the faithful are not immune to trauma?

When Solomon wrote that proverb, he wasn't talking about being righteous and blameless—he was talking about wisdom. The point he was making was that listening to wisdom creates a safer, less fearful future.

What Scripture does say about trauma is this: "In this world you *will* have trouble. But take heart! I have overcome the world" (John 16:33). These are the words of

Jesus, who was no stranger to trauma. He spoke this truth to His disciples, knowing full well they were about to experience the world-altering trauma of losing their friend in an unexpected, brutal tragedy. Jesus knew His friends would experience grief, derision, and persecution. Some would even be imprisoned, tortured, and killed. He told them they would suffer for a time but that their grief would one day turn to joy.

Knowing He was about to suffer the biggest big "T" Trauma of all and knowing His friends would not be able or willing to walk through that trauma with Him, Jesus reassured them, "Yet I am not alone, for my Father is with me" (John 16:32).

NOTHING IS TOO BIG TO HANDLE . . . *FOR GOD*

We often hear people say, "God won't give us more than we can handle." Some even believe this is a quote from the Bible. That statement isn't in the Bible. A lovely thought, but untrue. And unrealistic. We're constantly confronted with more than we can handle . . . on our own.

The true promise is this: There's nothing God can't handle. Nothing, nothing, absolutely nothing is too difficult for Him (Jeremiah 32:17). What we will not face is a trial, challenge, or sorrow that is too much for *Him*.

> *The true promise is this: There's nothing God can't handle.*

Sometimes we experience trauma that far exceeds what we are humanly capable of handling. I did. Maybe you have, or you currently are. In those times, we cry out to the Lord and ask Him to carry us through; we ask Him to help us survive. The promise from God is not that bad things won't happen. It is that He will never leave us to deal with those things by ourselves. God is always with us.

Listen to the psalmist's words in Psalm 34:18: "The LORD is close to the broken-hearted and saves those who are crushed in spirit." When we are broken and crushed like my little pear tree, the Lord is there to comfort, encourage, strengthen, and heal us.

Survival was the first priority for the pear tree, but it was not the endgame. The same is true for us. We will see that *it is not enough to simply survive*. God wants much more for us than that.

Questions for Reflection

1. Have you ever experienced big "T" Trauma? If you feel comfortable, jot down a sentence or two that describes that event.

2. If you're able, list two or three times in life when you have experienced little "t" trauma.

I have told you these things, so that in me you may have peace. In this world you will have trouble. But take heart! I have overcome the world.

JOHN 16:33

CHAPTER 2

When Dreams Die

*A*s mentioned in chapter 1, trauma always involves loss. Often trauma involves the loss of our most precious expectations for the future. Just as I had expectations that my pear tree would be the first to blossom in the spring and the last to drop its brightly colored leaves in the fall, we all have expectations for bright and beautiful things in our future.

In marriage, we may have plans to raise a family, travel, settle into a certain community, retire to a new location, grow old with our partner by our side, and so on. The trauma of divorce or a spouse's death brings these expectations to a grinding halt. A person is forced to reevaluate his or her goals and dreams for the future. When a spouse dies or a divorce takes place, vision for the future is lost. This is a loss that must be grieved before we can find hope in planning for a new future vision.

WHEN FUTURE DREAMS MUST CHANGE

As a therapist, I often talk with clients who are grieving the loss of an expected future. One of the most profound of such losses is the loss of a child. What parent doesn't begin to dream the minute he or she discovers a new child will be joining the family . . . or even before? We think about what our child will look like, how this little person will change the family, how intelligent our daughter will be, what kind of adult our son will grow into. We imagine ways this new human being might change the world, or at least our own world.

When a young life ends, what is a parent to do with all the expectations and dreams that were so acutely alive?

While I have not experienced the loss of a child myself, I have walked with parents on their grief journeys. My observations are simply that—observations. Many parents have expressed that the loss of a child is like a sudden, violent, head-on collision. The family is riding along, enjoying the view, when suddenly they hit a solid brick wall and everything comes to a devastating stop.

More than one grieving parent has told me, in both my professional and personal worlds, that losing a child makes ordinary life an offense. Have you heard or seen something like this? "How dare people carry on as if nothing earth-shattering happened in our family? Their worlds are still spinning. Mine stopped. Changed forever. They're going to work, to the gym, to church . . . and my life has come to a standstill. I know I shouldn't hold it against the non-grieving, but I can't help it."

Parents like this are clearly in the mire of the depression and anger phases of grief. Their expectations for their child and for the future of their family have been shattered. They can't imagine an alternative picture.

WHEN DOES FOREVER END?

My dear friends Dawn and Larry have experienced the loss of not one but two of their children. Dawn and Larry are kind, loving people who open their hearts and home to many. Although they both had been brought up in churchgoing families, each had difficult experiences growing up that resulted in a lack of understanding the true character of God. Both had rejected the idea of a loving God. They believed they could enjoy life and success without the baggage of religion.

After a few years of marriage, Dawn gave birth to Melissa, a beautiful little girl who from an early age had an uncanny sense of humor. When they discovered they were pregnant with baby number two, it seemed their expectations for having a happy family were well on their way to coming true.

After a healthy pregnancy, Dawn went into labor. The birth process progressed smoothly as the parents eagerly waited to greet their son, whom they had already named Daniel. But as soon as Daniel was born, he was whisked away. Something was terribly wrong.

The doctor quietly explained that a serious heart defect had been detected. Though a team of doctors worked diligently to save Daniel's life, he lived only three days.

After losing Daniel, Dawn and Larry were surrounded with support. Their needs were met consistently. Financial help arrived that just covered their deficits—no more, no less. It was undeniable that God was aware of their needs and was intervening to care for them.

Over the months that followed, Dawn felt an urgency to learn all she could about God. It wasn't long before she made a commitment to Him. She and Larry continued to grieve and struggled to understand each other's ways of grieving. This took a toll on their marriage and ultimately resulted in Dawn's spiraling into deep depression.

Dawn and Larry eventually gave birth to a second son, Nathan. Balancing the grief of losing Daniel and the joy of adding Nathan to the family created a unique combination of conflicting feelings. Larry became interested in knowing more about God, hoping also to make sense of this dichotomy of emotions. After months of study and prayer, he realized that some mysteries in life will never be understood by human beings. He longed to believe in a God who understood his pain, and soon he committed his life to Jesus.

Although life was not always easy, the family knew they were never alone. Nathan studied music in college and became the director of technology arts in a large church. Melissa completed her studies to be a nurse, but health issues began to plague her as she struggled to complete her twelve-hour shifts.

When Melissa entered her thirties, her health issues became more severe. Soon she was no longer able to work. She was losing the ability to walk and the strength to navigate her surroundings. Eventually she was diagnosed with myositis, a rare disease that attacked her muscles and organs. By the time Melissa was thirty-seven, the disease had become more than her body could bear, and she passed away.

After Melissa died, her mom found these words written on Melissa's bathroom mirror: *Lord, give me the faith to have hope.* Though fear of the unknown had challenged her resolve at times, Melissa knew there *was* hope, even if her body did not remain alive.

Dawn and Larry had now lost a second child. Through the years, they had grown close to Jesus and developed tremendous faith. But this did not give them immunity from the grief process. Denial, anger, bargaining, depression, and acceptance were still a part of their journey.

I once asked Dawn and Larry if grieving Daniel was different from grieving Melissa. Dawn's face lit up with a tender smile. "Oh, yes! So very different." She went on to say that she and Larry had grown apart after losing Daniel. They were both drowning in their individual grief and unable to face their loss as a couple. She described the unbearable depression that followed and the hopelessness she experienced. Because Dawn and Larry had no knowledge of or belief in heaven when they lost Daniel, the hopelessness they experienced was debilitating. Processing Daniel's loss was chaotic, with no "true north" to focus on in the process.

Melissa's death triggered the hopeless emotions that had been associated with Daniel's passing, but Dawn and Larry's definition of *forever* had since changed.

When Daniel passed, they believed they would grieve his loss forever. Lacking faith in God at that time, *forever* to them meant the rest of their lives followed by . . . nothing. No future, no hope, nothing. But with Melissa's passing years later, now as believers in Jesus, Dawn and Larry understood that they would *not* grieve forever. One day they would be reunited with their children in heaven and enjoy an *eternal forever* that would far exceed the number of days they'd missed with their children in this lifetime. Dawn and Larry found themselves reprocessing the grief related to Daniel's death, now in a healthier way, while also processing the loss of Melissa.

Because Dawn and Larry now shared the same faith and belief in eternal life, they were able to support one another in grief. They did not pull away from each other like they had when Daniel died. They focused on Jesus, prayed together, and reassured each other as they processed the loss of both children.

The couple found great assurance in knowing that Daniel and Melissa are free of pain, free of depression, and thriving in the presence of Jesus. Dawn said, "Our grief is still devastating, but we find comfort knowing we will see both Melissa and Daniel again one day. We cling to that hope and rejoice for both Melissa and Daniel."

Understanding and believing that this life is temporary and that we have hope for eternal life shifts our perception of forever. While this belief doesn't remove our grief, it adds hope to the journey. Our dreams for the future are not limited to this life we are living on earth. We can dream beyond life as we know it.

CHANGE IN PERSPECTIVE

First Thessalonians 4:13–14 says, "We do not want you to be uninformed, brothers, about those who are asleep [who have died], that you may not grieve as others do who have no hope. For since we believe that Jesus died and rose again, even so, through Jesus, God will bring with him those who have fallen asleep" (ESV).

These verses clearly state that grief is different for the believer. Grief without Jesus is hopeless, but with Jesus the perspective shifts and hope abounds.

When trauma steals our future dreams, there is still hope! God will not give us more than *He* can handle. God is working within both Dawn and Larry to reframe the hopeless emotions of Daniel's death, infusing in them the hope they have clung to since Melissa passed.

> *Grief without Jesus is hopeless, but with Jesus the perspective shifts and hope abounds.*

The loss of a child is just one example of trauma that causes us to lose future plans and visions. This is an example of a big "T" Trauma that is life-altering, but many forms of trauma change our expectations for the future.

Divorce, the loss of a job, conflict that undermines our reputation, a debilitating injury . . . whatever the circumstance, our perspective can have an enormous impact on how well we navigate healing from destroyed expectations. For Larry and Dawn, the hope of eternity in heaven didn't eliminate their grief and remove the trauma, but it softened the blow.

First John 3:20 says, "If our hearts condemn us, we know that God is greater than our hearts, and he knows everything." In Job 37:23 we find these words: "We cannot imagine the power of the Almighty; but even though he is just and righteous, he does not destroy us" (NLT). These two verses and many others in the Bible tell us that God knows everything and has complete power. Trusting in a God who is all-knowing and all-powerful is such a comfort. God's view of everything is much larger than the view from our personal vantage point. When we lose a job, God knows what is waiting for us in the future. When we face divorce, God still promises that He has a plan for us. When reputations are tarnished and damaged,

God still knows who we are and loves us without condition. Learning to trust God changes our perspective on literally everything.

His vision is complete. His provision is limitless. His plans will be fulfilled. His love is unchanging.

Questions for Reflection

1. What are your personal thoughts on eternity?

2. How might an eternal perspective change the way in which you process trauma that threatens future expectations?

This is the promise that he made to us—eternal life.

1 JOHN 2:25 (ESV)

CHAPTER 3

Taproots—Coping Strengths We Are Born With

*O*ur little pear tree looked pathetic. The tall trunk had two opposing, blunt-ended sticks poking awkwardly out from the top, which didn't look like sturdy enough branches for a small bird to land on safely. I was not sure these sticks would even qualify as branches. But as summer progressed, tiny green leaves began to form on those two orphaned sticks. My husband was quick to point this out.

"See?" he said. "The tree is fine. It has leaves."

I replied, "I would hardly say it's fine. Look at that thing!"

"Lisa, where is your faith? This tree comes from a tree farm with a great reputation. It was bred to be strong and full. It was well cared for during its first year, and all that care has strengthened its trunk. I think you are underestimating the potential that exists in this tree."

I closed my mouth, tended to the tree, and prayed for healing—although I was not confident that praying for God to heal a tree was good theological practice. And I rolled my eyes at my husband's comment when his back was turned.

By that time, I had lived with the subconscious aftereffects of big "T" Trauma for decades. It disturbed my sleep, kept me hyperalert to my surroundings, and, despite the efforts I'll describe a little later, in chapter 13, altered the way I looked at almost everything, from rooms to doors to beds to campuses to touch.

When I looked at the tree, some part of my brain saw *me* all those years ago.

I decided I would go through the motions of nurturing this dead sapling, mostly so my husband would realize the horrific consequences of his actions when it inevitably proved impossible. He had killed our tree. Of this I was certain.

Most of us who have experienced big "T" Trauma or chronic little "t" trauma understand what it feels like to just go through the motions. We do what we need to in order to keep putting one foot in front of the other, but it feels inauthentic and meaningless. I nurtured the tree even though I thought my care was pointless and wouldn't help.

STRONG TAPROOTS

An oak tree doesn't begin to produce acorns until twenty to fifty years after its life cycle commences. Each acorn only contains one seed, but one tree can produce thousands of acorns. When the fallen acorn seed germinates, it produces a taproot that will anchor the new tree for the rest of its life. Once spring arrives, that taproot sends up a shoot, which produces leaves that reach for the sun and begin the process of photosynthesis.

Keep in mind that the taproot forms before the seedling even begins to emerge. The anchor is set, and the tree's strength is predetermined to some extent by what happens prior to the birth of the seedling.

When we are born, we too have already begun the process of establishing traits that will anchor us in life. Some of us are natural peacemakers. Some are born with strong resolve. Others are born with a calm demeanor that is not easily shaken. We are all born with specific strengths and weaknesses, and these traits begin to be challenged by the world around us from the moment we are born. Our character traits are a result of nature, and we can learn to use our natural strengths to cope with difficult situations. Unfortunately, those strong traits we are born with can also work against us when unmanaged.

SAM'S STORY

"Sam" was born addicted to drugs. Sam's birth mother had struggled with addiction. She either didn't have the taproots she needed to hold her steady when challenges entered her life or had something that kept her from learning to use her taproots effectively. Shortly after giving birth, Sam's birth mother abandoned him at the hospital.

Sam had experienced trauma before his seedling self even emerged, so he started his seedling life in a vulnerable state. He would tremble and cry inconsolably as his little body worked its way through the symptoms of withdrawal. The hospital staff that cared for Sam made sure he was as comfortable as possible. They would rock him, gently stroke him, and swaddle him as he gained tolerance of touch and movement.

> *We can learn to use our natural strengths to cope with difficult situations.*

"Claire" and "Ryan," a couple licensed in foster care for infants, were contacted. They agreed to prepare a home for Sam while he was healing in the hospital. Claire and Ryan visited Sam every day and spent time rocking him, feeding him, and praying that he would feel the love they showered upon him.

Little Sam remained in the hospital for six weeks. As the withdrawal symptoms subsided, Claire and Ryan increased the level of physical nurturing they provided. By the time they brought Sam home from the hospital, he seemed comfortable and at ease with them. A crying Sam could be comforted by the sound of Claire's gentle voice or by Ryan's soft beard rubbing against his cheek.

The foster parents bonded with Sam from the first days of his life, and he eventually bonded with them. It wasn't long before Claire and Ryan petitioned the court to adopt Sam. By the time he was a year old, they were officially a family.

As beautiful as this story is, Sam's difficult time in the womb affected his taproots. Sam could be comforted by his adoptive parents, but he was unable to console himself when he was agitated. He would cry nonstop when he was not being held.

Claire and Ryan found themselves exhausted as they provided undivided attention all day for Sam and then were awakened each night by his fearful cries. Sleep-deprived and unable to focus on self-care, the parents were visibly weary. But they were hesitant to speak negatively of their new son or about the difficulties in their new little family. They bragged about their Sam, focusing only on the positive.

Claire saw how special Sam was, having survived more than most adults experience in a lifetime. She felt guilty for being impatient or frustrated in caring for him. She thought he deserved only the best, and that she was failing him as a mom.

Ryan also felt like he was not living up to his potential as a father for Sam. He imagined coming home from work, helping with dinner and household chores, and then playing and laughing with his son. But in reality, he dreaded going home after work, knowing that he'd be caring for a fussy infant all night.

Claire and Ryan saw their innocent son as a blank slate, and they saw their job being to write love, joy, and contentment into his life. They experienced guilt about feeling anything to the contrary.

Guilt, however, was not theirs to carry.

Yes, Sam was innocent, but he was not a blank slate. He had already experienced trauma before he was born, and he'd been strong enough to thrive in the womb, even though his mother's body had not provided for his needs. He was strong enough to battle through the symptoms of withdrawal and strong enough to thrive physically, despite the challenges he was born with.

Like an acorn that was planted in poor soil, Sam had developed taproots before he ever came into this world. Sam was born with a fighting spirit and a strong will. These characteristics had helped him to survive thus far, but they also contributed to his ability to throw a proper temper tantrum. He had capitalized on strength but had not learned to calm himself. Self-soothing was a coping skill he had yet to learn, and it would take time for him to do so.

His adoptive parents had been born with taproots as well. Both were intelligent, compassionate, and resourceful. Claire had been blessed with a patient and calm demeanor, and Ryan was energetic and goal oriented. Claire was a nurse but was staying home to care for Sam. Ryan was an engineer. His job was fast-paced and required his full attention during the day, but work was left at work so that he could devote all his time and energy to Claire and Sam when he was home.

It was important for Claire and Ryan to know they, too, had strong taproots. If they could identify how they were wired, they could figure out what resources would be of most help to them. We are anchored by characteristics that are trustworthy, steadfast, and never changing. For example, Claire was a rational voice of reason in most cases. She was patient and loving, even under pressure. Ryan was known to be a hard worker, and provided support for his family both financially and emotionally. These are characteristics that would help the family over time.

Ryan was a morning person and Claire was energized late into the night. It was possible to schedule certain routine chores and responsibilities accordingly. In addition, Claire enjoyed prepping food for Sam, and Ryan enjoyed bathing Sam and putting him to bed at night. Understanding each other's strengths and weaknesses as well as likes and dislikes would help the couple balance the load a bit.

Perhaps the greatest challenge for this couple was finding rest. They were both standing in the same rocky soil of raising a child who required more attention than most. They were in need of external resources too. One such resource was a trusted person who could take care of Sam, allowing the parents some time for self-care. They discovered a teen neighbor who loved to play with Sam. The sitter was able to give her undivided attention to Sam when visiting, and Sam enjoyed playing with her. This time was good for Sam, and it was good for his parents. Claire and Ryan needed time to rest and recharge. These are basic human needs.

Claire and Ryan hired the babysitter to play with Sam once a week while they enjoyed a dinner out. This gave them time to enjoy each other's company and recharge their batteries while knowing that Sam was being well taken care of. When they would pick Sam up from the babysitter's, they had the energy to enjoy Sam's bath time, read him books, and help him peacefully fall asleep in his own bed.

Over time, Claire and Ryan discovered that Sam's strong character would serve him well. He slowly began to play independently. Although he was sometimes demanding, he was also able to find ways to occupy himself when his parents were not readily available to play with him.

Other innate traits worked in his favor as well. He was intelligent and sensitive to the feelings of others. At the age of four he could notice when his mom was having a difficult day. Sometimes he would pat her on the back and say, "It's okay, Mommy. I love you." Claire would laugh about his big-boy interactions, but these actions were a sign that he was learning to use his taproots in a mature way.

Over the years, Claire and Ryan also identified ways to use their taproots to face challenging times. They were blessed with characteristics that were strong and sure. Some of the common characteristics this couple shared were a high level of emotional intelligence, a strong work ethic, and a compassionate disposition.

Claire and Ryan prayed daily together and with Sam. They enlisted the help of friends from church when they were overwhelmed. Sam was able to attend Sunday school with people whom he had known since birth, so this became an activity he could look forward to each week. All these resources were dependable, stable, and unwavering. In this way, Claire and Ryan found that they could utilize the taproots of others to manage the load. People often enjoy the opportunity to share their gifts and talents with others.

Raising Sam wasn't without its challenges, but I am happy to report Sam grew up to be a healthy, loving human being. Despite the challenges he was born with, his taproots held firm, and his parents helped nurture his character so those taproots would continue to support him for the rest of his life.

IDENTIFY YOUR TAPROOTS

Imagine if Claire and Ryan had given up. Sam might have been passed from foster home to foster home with no consistent guidance or nourishment for his taproots. His strength of character could have taken him to some very dark places.

We all have that potential.

It can be extremely helpful to identify the personality traits we were born with as we consider our own struggles after trauma. Knowing our strengths helps us determine what we need in our healing process. For example, an extrovert who typically loves to be around people would probably not benefit from isolation for extended periods of time. Although an extrovert may be tempted to isolate, he or she will likely find it helpful to connect with friends and loved ones while processing the trauma. Someone who enjoys creative pursuits might find it helpful to write, draw, or use music as a healing tool. It might even be helpful to ask others what they see as your strong character traits and discuss how those traits may help or hinder your moving forward.

> *Knowing our strengths helps us determine*
> *what we need in our healing process.*

When you are exhausted and don't feel strong, allow others to step in and use the gifts they have to help. If you need to talk, call a friend who is wired to listen. If you need rest, let someone take some of your load for a bit.

Following trauma, we may fear that our strengths are being challenged and will not hold up. For example, a person who prizes his or her ability to think logically may struggle with the chaotic, nonsensical nature of trauma. Logic may feel completely out of reach, and this can be debilitating to an analytical thinker. Yet over time, that same logic may be helpful in walking through the traumatic event. Remember, your trauma doesn't define you. The strengths that lived within you before trauma live within you still.

As you read through the following list of sample character traits, think of your personality prior to trauma. Who have you proven to be over time? Which traits served you well in the past, and which may have been problematic? You were born with qualities to help you in the healing process. Which of these characteristics have acted as taproots in your life?

☐ Adaptable	☐ Confident	☐ Energetic
☐ Ambitious	☐ Consistent	☐ Extroverted
☐ Bold	☐ Creative	☐ Fair
☐ Calm	☐ Disciplined	☐ Flexible
☐ Compassionate	☐ Encouraging	☐ Goal oriented

☐ Honest   ☐ Loyal   ☐ Reliable

☐ Independent   ☐ Mild mannered   ☐ Resilient

☐ Insightful   ☐ Optimistic   ☐ Resourceful

☐ Introverted   ☐ Patient   ☐ Responsible

☐ Logical   ☐ Persistent   ☐ Social

This is not an exhaustive list. Can you think of other personality traits that are unique to you? Feel free to add them. I hope this begins a process of understanding what coping skills you were created with.

LEAN ON THE UNWAVERING CHARACTER OF GOD

The most persistent, reliable, trustworthy resource I have found in life is the Word of God. Scripture has existed for millennia, unchanged, yet it still speaks to our modern-day challenges and provides support, encouragement, and advice that have withstood the test of time.

Hebrews 6:17–19 says, "Because God wanted to make the unchanging nature of his purpose very clear to the heirs of what was promised, he confirmed it with an oath. God did this so that, by two unchangeable things in which it is impossible for God to lie, we who have fled to take hold of the hope set before us may be greatly encouraged. We have this hope as an anchor for the soul, firm and secure."

Hope is what anchors our souls. The resources we count on in life should be ones that offer hope for a rich and blessed future as opposed to ones that offer false security and false hope.

Anchoring yourself in the Word of God can be done in a number of ways. For Claire and Ryan, joining a Bible study for parents of young children became a valuable resource. Together, these parents found nuggets of information to encourage them in parenting. They were able to share the joys and challenges of being parents and offer ideas and godly support to one another.

A group Bible study has many advantages. However, following trauma, you may not feel up to meeting with others or diving deeply into a study. That's okay—you can start with small steps. We will discuss some simple ways to build your relationship with God in chapter 13, but for now, consider getting a devotional and reading one short message each day, or ask friends to share meaningful Scripture verses with you and read one daily. Even a line or two of Scripture can be of great encouragement.

Questions for Reflection

1. How might others describe your personality? What taproots may contribute to those perceptions?

2. What needs do you have right now that are difficult to carry alone? Think of someone who naturally has the skills to help you carry the load.

We have this hope as an anchor for the soul, firm and secure.

HEBREWS 6:19

CHAPTER 4

Root Systems—Coping Strengths We Develop

Trees form root systems early in life. The deeper the root system, the stronger the plant. The most readily accessible water and nutrients are found near the top of the soil and shallow roots can access these nutrients to sustain life on a day-to-day basis, but if a tree grows only shallow, wide roots, what happens when a drought occurs or a heavy storm arises? During a drought, the water on top of the ground dries up and the soil quality is destroyed. Those shallow roots cannot find the nutrients and water needed to support the life of the tree. And if a storm produces high winds, the shallow roots will not be strong enough to hold the tree upright.

When either Big "T" or little "t" trauma threatens to fell us, shallow roots—those that help us survive at a basic level—are not enough to sustain us or allow us to grow in strength.

Deeper roots not only have the reach to access deeper reservoirs of water but also store water farther underground for later access during dry seasons. Deep roots strengthen the tree at all times but become even more efficient and important when conditions become harsh.

What are the roots we grow as human beings? What holds us solid, keeps nourishing us, and maintains our stability when harsh conditions come along?

MEETING NEEDS GROWS STRONGER ROOTS

Maslow's hierarchy of needs defines basic needs that must be met for human beings to survive, grow, and thrive. We can look to this simple model to determine where to focus our energy in growing roots. For the sake of comparing this triangle to the root systems of plants, let's turn it upside down. (No worries, Maslow, we can put it back when we finish here.)

Maslow's Hierarchy of Needs

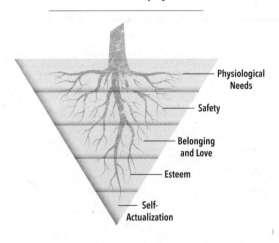

The most basic needs must be met in order for a person to survive. These are physiological and tangible: food, water, air to breathe, rest, and shelter from the elements. When a parent meets these needs in a baby, the baby will live. If a baby's physiological needs are not provided for immediately, human life ends. This continues to be the case throughout life, though as we grow, we depend less on our caretakers to provide our basic needs and learn to provide for ourselves.

As we get deeper into the soil of life, we find the need for safety. Again, as infants we typically count on parents or caretakers to meet this need. A baby can be well fed, warm, and rested, but if left in otherwise dangerous circumstances, his or her life could be threatened. Even as adults, we can find our sense of safety threatened, but as we age, we'll ideally become more independent in protecting ourselves and getting ourselves into safer situations. When we trust that we are safe, our roots continue to grow.

These first two levels of Maslow's hierarchy make up our basic human needs. When they are met, life is sustainable. These are the shallow, broad roots that allow us to survive.

As we mature, we send our roots down even deeper, to the needs for belonging and love. These deeper needs relate to the psyche, and help us to not only survive but grow. These needs are met through intimate relationships, family bonding, and friendships. Strong relationships are how we develop our support system. People who don't know who to reach out to in times of distress often feel unloved and disconnected. Sadly, many who commit suicide feel this need is not met for them. That doesn't mean that in fact no one loves them; it means they *perceive* they are not loved and cared for. Perceived connection to others is critical to survival during times of crisis.

Once a person feels connected to others, roots reach down to the next level of need—esteem. Often I hear people say, "I don't care what others think of me." That, to me, is a telltale sign that they do care. Maslow makes clear that it is an actual human need to be viewed in a positive light by other people—and by ourselves as well. We need to feel accomplished in our own eyes, to believe we are making a difference in the world.

When we doubt our own self-worth, we look outside ourselves for positive feedback and praise. It takes a deep, strong root system to develop true *self*-esteem, the ability to be confident in who we are despite what others might think. For those who grow such healthy roots, statements like "I don't care what others think of me" don't even occur to them because they aren't distracted by how others perceive them.

> *Often I hear people say, "I don't care what others think of me." That is a telltale sign that they do care.*

Now for the deepest roots of all. Maslow suggests that the highest-level need of the human psyche is self-actualization. Meeting this need means that a human being feels enabled to achieve their full potential in every way. Self-actualization is not about surviving but about thriving.

Isn't that the goal of every human being? Thriving? It is simply not enough to just survive, is it?

When we imagine our human root system as a metaphor for Maslow's triangle, we see that the deeper our roots, the stronger we become. When trauma occurs, we count on our root system to hold.

OBSTACLES TO DEEP GROWTH

Unfortunately, many obstacles can arise to stunt the growth of our root system. A tree planted in shallow soil can send roots only so deep. If the bedrock is close to the surface, for example, the roots must expand outward rather than downward. But remember, while wide, shallow roots will help meet the tree's basic survival needs, they will not hold up in harsh conditions. Depth is needed for persistence and flourishing. It is much the same for us.

Many things in life can hinder root growth. Perhaps an infant's parents or caretakers are unable or unwilling to meet the child's basic needs. When a baby's most basic needs go unmet, even if that infant survives, the crucial parent-child bond never gets established, and the child is unable to grow his or her roots deeper. Adults who went without that bond during infancy face a lifetime of difficulty.

Obstacles can arrive at any phase in life, and trauma can interrupt our growth in dramatic ways. A house fire or natural disaster might shake our confidence that our physiological needs will be met. Witnessing or experiencing a violent crime may damage our perception of safety. Infidelity or divorce can set us back dramatically in our need for love and belonging.

Almost nothing can stop the growth of deep roots more quickly or completely than childhood sexual abuse (CSA). Many, if not all, of our basic needs are to be met by our parents or caretakers early in life, yet for many children, it is these very people who violate their safety. Perpetrated by a parent or caretaker, CSA catastrophically damages a child's sense of security. Inflicted by someone other than a caretaker, CSA plants seeds of doubt in a young heart. The child will wonder who, if anyone, can keep them safe.

But the shattering, root-destroying impact of sexual abuse isn't limited to childhood events only.

TWO ROOT-DEPTH CASE STUDIES

Let's take a look at two hypothetical situations and how root systems might impact healing. Two women, both members of the armed services, had experienced sexual assault while deployed. Both were diagnosed with PTSD. (We will talk more about that diagnosis in a later chapter.)

These were capable women who had stepped into the military with high hopes of fulfilling careers. Each woman was physically strong and extremely intelligent.

"Theresa" was nineteen when she was deployed overseas and tasked with ordering and maintaining supplies for her regiment. She had entered the military at eighteen, partially to escape a difficult home life. Theresa had been raised by a single mom who struggled financially and was both physically and emotionally absent. At age eight, Theresa became responsible for the care of her two younger siblings. But when Theresa became a teenager, her mother married for the first time. Suddenly Theresa was not the caretaker.

Her stepfather was a controlling and difficult man who wanted to be in charge always. He and Theresa often clashed when she attempted to parent her siblings, as was her habit. Although the stepfather provided more financial stability in the home, his violent temper caused much anxiety.

Theresa had learned to provide for her own physiological needs at a young age, which likely created insecurities for her early on. She had strong taproots of persistence and determination, and she very likely learned to be resourceful. But her basic needs for belonging and safety were compromised.

"Elise" was twenty-two when she was deployed. With a bachelor's degree in communications, she was directly involved in intelligence. Elise grew up in a typical middle-class family. Her mother was an aesthetician, and her father owned a contracting company. Elise also had two younger siblings, both of whom were in college.

Elise's family was close-knit, and her parents worked very hard to make sure their children would have the opportunity to go to college one day. Elise had made the decision to join the Reserve Officers' Training Corps (ROTC) when she entered college because she knew she'd be able to use her education to serve her country and also because paying off student loans would be easier with military deferment.

Neither Elise nor Theresa could have anticipated what lay ahead. Each woman experienced sexual violence within a month of deployment. But while they both reported the crime to their superiors, neither was successful in finding justice. Instead, the women's reports only exposed them to ridicule and pressure within the ranks.

After reporting her experience, Theresa was medically discharged from the service for mental health reasons. Following her assault, Theresa had turned to alcohol to numb her pain. She had begun drinking so heavily that she was unable to perform her duties and was deemed no longer deployable.

Elise remained in the service after reporting the crime against her. She was functioning satisfactorily but struggling with sleep disturbances, flashbacks, and dissatisfaction with her position. Elise continued to work and pursue her hobbies, but she was often exhausted. She also dealt with depression.

Elise found ways to reframe the things that caused her stress. For example, she was triggered when she was called in to meetings with her supervisor. She would worry that each meeting carried bad news. With the help of a therapist, she was able to reframe this by telling herself that meetings with her supervisor were an inevitable, necessary part of her job, and that her new supervisor was positive and encouraging. She also found the confidence to speak openly with her new superior officers about her experience. As a result, her supervisors worked with her to avoid triggering situations in her workspace. Over time, she made the decision to leave the armed services.

Theresa sought therapy to help cope with her anxiety. She was able to achieve a year of sobriety but continued to struggle with panic attacks, family conflict, and flashbacks. As a result of her dysfunction, she was placed on permanent disability. Theresa will likely attend AA and require therapy for a very long time.

What is the difference between Theresa and Elise? They have completely different root systems and taproots.

Theresa's holistic needs as a child were not met by her caretakers. Her mother provided the basic needs of food, water, and shelter, but she did not bond with Theresa in a loving, protective way. Instead, Theresa's mother counted on Theresa to protect and provide for her siblings. Because of that chaotic environment, Theresa was not close to her family and never developed a strong support system. Lacking were the deep roots that could have provided stability when she faced trauma as a teen. And the assault itself blocked Theresa's roots from growing deeper to include esteem or self-actualization. Unfortunately, she also struggled to employ her own taproots. Theresa was born with character traits that may have served her well, but she turned to alcohol as a way to numb her pain. Numbing pain does not lead to healing.

Is healing out of reach for Theresa? No. Healing is possible for everyone. There is still hope for Theresa. Her dependence on alcohol simply created another obstacle for her to overcome. We will look into obstacles to healing more in chapter 6.

Elise, on the other hand, had developed a deep, strong root system. Her family was close, and her friendships were very tight. When she was assaulted, she had many people she could trust and depend on. Her family and friends encouraged her to seek help, which she did with confidence while still enlisted. Elise also had a strong sense of her own identity and worth. As a believer in Jesus, she found comfort and strength in prayer even when she felt vulnerable during her deployment.

For better or worse, our childhood experiences prepare us for future storms in life, including trauma. In therapy we identify the negative thoughts we might have about ourselves, often instilled at a young age, and try to replace them with positive cognitions that strengthen our ability to cope with tough and traumatic situations. We then use the resources we have already developed in life, like sense of identity and support from others, to truly believe the positive things about ourselves. Both Theresa and Elise were working toward goals of personal strength; one simply had more resources to bring to the table.

RESOURCES TO HELP US ALONG THE WAY

As children, we hope parents will be providers, protectors, and sustainers of life. As adults, recognizing God as our ultimate resource brings lasting security.

Why is this important? Because human beings are not perfect, nor are they infallibly dependable. Humans have limits to what they can do for others. We even have expiration dates! God, however, is unlimited in power, strength, love, time, purpose, and so on.

It's often said that difficult times make us stronger. Unfortunately, this is only true for those who have a strong root system. Those with a shallow root system are far more likely to buckle under pressure and to suffer from depression, anxiety, and addiction. Some will even resort to suicide.

If you didn't grow up with circumstances that helped you to grow a deep root system, I want to encourage you. You *can* continue to grow these roots throughout life. Many people learn to do so through therapy and attending programs like Alcoholics Anonymous or Celebrate Recovery. If your childhood involved dysfunction that stunted your root growth, there is hope. Many have discovered ways to overcome a rough start in life. It is my prayer that you will feel confident in growing deeper roots as you continue to read.

Questions for Reflection

1. Think about your own root system. What needs were met for you as a child? What areas may need further growth?

2. Make a list of unmet needs in your life. Pray over this list, asking God to meet your needs and to grow your roots more deeply.

They will be like a tree planted by the water that sends out its roots by the stream. It does not fear when heat comes; its leaves are always green. It has no worries in a year of drought and never fails to bear fruit.

JEREMIAH 17:8

CHAPTER 5

Surviving the Immediate Aftermath of Trauma

So far we have been talking about characteristics and learned skills we hope to develop before we face trauma. Both having had our basic needs met at an early age and learning to employ the strong character traits we were born with can help us in the recovery process.

The needs of those who experience trauma change over time. At first, meeting our most basic needs will be our priority, but as we face the reality of our trauma, building relationships to lean on will become a necessity as well. Also, to truly move into a place of healing, we will need to progress and find resilience, hope, a sense of purpose, and even joy.

We'll start that progression in this chapter, where we'll talk about what can be done immediately following a traumatic event. During this phase, there is confusion and emotional distress. We are often unable to make clear decisions and plans to move forward. When chaos surrounds us, our five senses become overloaded with information. We rely on our senses to process what is going on around us, and when this overload occurs, it's as if our wiring gets scrambled, and therefore we have a hard time making logical connections.

> *When chaos surrounds us, our five senses become overloaded with information.*

In the immediate aftermath of trauma, basic needs take precedence. As we learned from Maslow in the previous chapter, physiological and safety needs top the list. We'll explore how this principle plays out in situations of mass trauma, and then we'll look at how to apply these steps to more personal traumatic events.

MASS TRAUMA

Stories in earlier chapters pertained to personal experiences, including loss of loved ones and sexual assault, but sometimes trauma impacts large populations of people, as is the case with natural disasters. In personal experiences of trauma, we hope someone nearby can comfort and care for those who have been traumatized. But sometimes the trauma is so widespread that everyone in the vicinity is experiencing it at the same time. Such events can lead to even more chaos, confusion, and overload.

During the summer of 2010, I had the opportunity to spend two weeks in Japan. After touring Kyoto and Tokyo, we took a bullet train north to Yahaba-Cho, a town in the Iwate Prefecture, where I stayed with a couple who were old enough to be my parents. We bonded very quickly despite the language differences.

These two weeks were part of a community exchange program. Our American delegation spent two weeks in Japan; then a delegation of residents from Japan spent two weeks in my hometown. This ongoing exchange forged friendships that were long-lasting and meaningful.

While in Japan, a group of friends, both Japanese and American, took a road trip along the Goishi Coast. We stopped to see the beautiful Anatoshi-Iso rock formations in Ofunato, where we also visited the gift shops and had lunch. From there we headed to a camp where we were supplied with life jackets and kayaks for a tour on the water. We kayaked into the bay to see up close the massive tsunami wall that had been erected to protect the town of Ofunato. The wall looked like a giant dam, and had a tall center seawall that could be raised and lowered using diesel generators. On this day the wall was raised and the ocean beyond was accessible and visible to us. In the case of a tsunami warning, the wall would be lowered so its massive size and strength would block potential damage to the city. The wall towered over us, seemingly impenetrable.

I learned much about earthquakes and tsunamis that day. And later in the week, we visited an earthquake center and experienced a simulated earthquake. We laughed as we tried to keep our balance in the shaking mock kitchen. Pots and pans flew off countertops and tripped up our footing. Afterward, a man told us that while the simulation seemed fun and silly, a real-life situation is terrifying and serious.

During our stay we experienced several small tremors that reminded us of the reality of earthquakes in that region. I confess that on my last day in Japan, I prayed that I might experience one *real* earthquake. I said, "God, I would love to know what an earthquake feels like. Might you allow one obvious but not dangerous shake before we leave?"

Guess what? God answered my prayer. As we prepared to head to the airport, the house began to shudder. I went downstairs to the kitchen and noticed that dishes were rattling in the cupboards. Outside the glass door I could see bundles of kindling rolling back and forth as the ground moved with more and more power. My host was outside in the middle of the street, waving at me and yelling my name. I waved back, thinking she was happy I was experiencing this event. I later learned she was calling me to the street, terrified that the house would fall on me. I was very naive in my ideas of earthquakes.

When I returned to the United States, I often thought of our day on the Goishi Coast and the friendships that had been forged in those short two weeks. Many of us stayed in touch through social media, and we enjoyed a visit when several of them came to the United States. It was less than a year later that I watched in horror as the news channels showed footage of the devastating 2011 Tohoku earthquake and the massive tsunami that struck Japan. Our US delegation tried desperately to find out if our friends were safe. Most of the Goishi Coast had been obliterated. Many days passed before we could connect with our friends, but we soon learned that the tsunami wall we had kayaked to crumbled under the force of the tsunami. The camp, the gift shop, the restaurant, and all the other places we had visited no longer existed. Thousands had died in the town of Ofunato alone.

We praised God when we learned that our camp tour guide was safe, but our hearts broke when we learned that his friends and his fiancée had never been found. The couple who had hosted me were in separate parts of Japan. The wife was safe at home, but her husband had traveled by bullet train to Tokyo for work, and she wasn't sure where he was. Parts of the bullet train had been washed away, and travel had come to a complete stop. The infrastructure in Japan was so devastated that communication was impossible for several days. It was more than a week before this precious family learned that all their loved ones had survived the disaster, and more than a month before they could be reunited. My hosts' son had survived the tsunami in Fukushima, but damage to the Fukushima Daiichi Nuclear Power Plant left the community vulnerable and residents in danger for years to come.

Little "t" Trauma of Observers

The trauma the other US delegates and I experienced during this time was little "t" trauma. We were able to call one another, share updates, and pray for our friends as we watched the devastation unfold on TV. Because we were not in physical danger and our basic needs were not in jeopardy, we could think rationally and even make plans for how we might help our friends moving forward.

Big "T" Trauma of Survivors

Our friends in Japan were experiencing big "T" Trauma in every way imaginable. Many were without shelter, transportation, and food. All were either in immediate danger or had family and loved ones who were. There was no way to communicate to see who was alive, who was injured, or who needed help. The chaos and terror would have been overwhelming. Remember that our five senses can be overloaded during trauma. What did these people see, hear, taste, smell, and feel? It is unfathomable for those of us who have never experienced such a catastrophic natural disaster.

Basic Needs and Local Support

In the immediate aftermath of natural disaster, remember that it is basic needs that need to be addressed first: food, shelter, water, medical attention, and safety. These are things most of us take for granted, so in this situation it will probably feel shocking to concentrate on these things. Everyone in the area will have experienced the same trauma at the same time, and all of them have the same needs. Outside help is needed as soon as possible, beginning with aid from those who live close to the destruction but still have access to necessities. These neighbors are probably also dealing with trauma and uncertainty, but they may be able to help provide resources for basic survival.

Agency Help and Psychological First Aid

Help may then come from agencies such as the Red Cross and other international relief organizations, humanitarian groups, and missions teams. Many of those responders will use psychological first aid (PFA). The purpose of PFA is to provide safety and to stabilize survivors. PFA can be provided by mental health professionals but also by other first responders. The process includes assessing the needs of survivors and helping them find resources to meet those needs.

Calming survivors who are too emotionally distraught to function is part of this ongoing work, but PFA is not the same as therapy. The objective of PFA is survival, not long-term healing.

Debriefing

Once safety and survival are secure, which can take anywhere from days to months, survivors will go through a period of debriefing. During this time, a trained facilitator, counselor, or volunteer leader will encourage survivors to share the details of their experience. Where were they? What did they see, hear, taste, smell, and feel? How did they respond? What emotions did they experience?

Debriefing helps make the traumatic experience more real and concrete. At first the experience is likely to feel surreal, like something seen in a movie. Distancing ourselves from the event in this way is called *dissociation*, a term I briefly mentioned in chapter 1. Dissociation is a natural instinct, a survival technique. Being able to remember the events as if they did not happen directly to us protects us emotionally for a time. Dissociation is healthy and normal at first; left unchecked, however, it can lead to mental health issues and can prevent healing over time. Eventually we need to face the reality of our trauma. Debriefing is the beginning of that process.

FOCUSING ON PERSONAL BIG "T" TRAUMA

We have considered the early phase of processing trauma: finding local support; meeting the basic needs of food, water, shelter, and medical attention; bringing in support from agencies and groups that can administer psychological first aid; and debriefing. It is easy to see how these steps are necessary following a broad-scale natural disaster—but how do they apply to big "T" Trauma experienced by individuals? Ask yourself the following questions and follow a similar pattern of action steps.

In the aftermath of trauma, to whom can you go for immediate assistance? Is there a friend you can call for help? Are there neighbors who can assist? Look for people who offer help, and be prepared to accept.

Next, are you getting nourishment? Trauma survivors often forget to eat and drink or just don't feel like doing so; if you are in this pattern, it is important that you recognize it and commit to eating a few times daily, even if it's just a few bites of protein. Ask for help with meals as well. People who bring you meals meet vital needs beyond the essentials of food and water—they also provide you with friendship and emotional support.

When trauma involves the loss of a home, finding shelter is primary. A house fire, separation, domestic abuse, child abuse . . . whatever the event, if the trauma happened in your home, you may not be prepared to return there right away. Where can you stay that offers shelter and safety for the time being?

Identify local agencies and resources that are equipped to offer assistance. You may need to call the police, go to the hospital, or find a social worker. What services are you aware of that assist others in your area with needs similar to yours?

Finally, you will need someone to debrief with. Local counselors are typically equipped to assist with this step, and first responders may be able to direct you to other resources for debriefing. It is important that you tell your story and face the reality of the trauma. Many people avoid talking about the incident, either because they don't want to be a burden, they are embarrassed, or they just don't want to think about it. But debriefing is an important early step in the healing process and should occur as soon as possible, once you're safe and in a stable location.

Basic needs. Psychological first aid. Debriefing. These steps are essential to navigating the immediate aftermath of any big "T" Trauma—whether it's a personal experience of trauma or a widespread event. Use these simple steps as a road map to get through this time.

> *Debriefing is an important early step in the healing process and should occur as soon as possible.*

Until help from others arrives, focus on meeting basic needs and supporting those near you. Debriefing may begin to occur naturally as you and others start to share your stories. If your trauma is a personal experience, allow others to guide you through this process. Avoiding these steps can hinder your ability to cope and move forward.

I know survival probably doesn't feel easy right now, but it is the first step on the journey. I promise you that better is to come. God will not abandon you in this crisis. As you read through this book, together we will walk through the journey from survival to encountering the goodness of God once again in this lifetime. One step at a time, my friend. You've got this.

Questions for Reflection

1. How did you feel supported the first few days after your greatest trauma?

2. What basic needs did (or do) you have?

Do not fear, for I am with you; do not be dismayed,
for I am your God. I will strengthen you and help you;
I will uphold you with my righteous right hand.

ISAIAH 41:10

CHAPTER 6

Avoiding Artificial Coping

A few weeks after my pear tree was ravaged by the ugly pine, my husband walked into the room with a Cheshire-cat smile on his face. I was sitting on the sofa, working on my computer. He fell into an armchair, allowing his hands to linger and then drop with a slap onto the armrests. I raised my eyes just above the computer screen and took in his grin.

"I just had the greatest idea of all time," he said. Pride was plastered on his face.

I sighed and tentatively asked, "Okay, what is it?" In my defense, his last greatest idea of all time was to bring an engine into our living room so he could work on it and still have family time. I was hesitant, to say the least.

He went on. "The leaves growing on the tree tell me that it isn't dead. It's just injured. I think I know how we can help it along." Barry went on to share his idea of splicing branches from various fruit trees into the perfect trunk of the pear tree to create a tree that would be full of branches. "The genius," he said, "is that each branch would flower in a different color and the tree would provide all different kinds of fruits. Picture it! We could grow apples, pears, cherries, peaches, and plums all on one tree!"

I shook my head in disbelief. "Are you serious?"

"I am completely serious! Our tree would be the most interesting tree around. It would be colorful and functional." His words were meant to convince me. They didn't.

"Barry, the branches would all be different shapes, and would bloom at different times. The colors would be a mismatched mess. It would be a Franken-tree. Is that representative of our blended family? Are we a Franken-family?"

"Of course not," he laughed. "I think it would be a fun experiment. It could be really pretty, and it would help the tree fill in."

Friends, I am going to tell you straight up, we did *not* decide to create a Franken-tree. Barry may have been right about one thing, though. The few green leaves poking out of its two remaining sticks might mean the tree wasn't dead after all. Its woundedness might not be its demise. I would nurture what was there and see what happened.

ARTIFICIAL COPING

When we are wounded by trauma, it might feel like we are dying and like we have no hope. But given time, if we persist in the healing process, we will begin to notice little signs of new life growing within us. But because the journey to healing is difficult and arduous, we might be tempted to try to splice things into our lives to speed the process. These artificial coping efforts can create a monster that interferes with true healing.

In the introduction to this book, I shared a poem called "Am I a Survivor?" I drew from a compilation of stories when I wrote that poem. My own story of struggling to see myself as a survivor inspired the poem, but I wrote the end of the poem based on the story of another woman. She too had been sexually assaulted, but she turned to an artificial coping method to help ease her pain. She became dependent on alcohol.

> *Artificial coping efforts can create a monster that interferes with true healing.*

This woman was a Christian, but she trusted alcohol to numb her pain more than she trusted that Jesus could heal it. She became so dependent on alcohol that she lost her job, her marriage, and custody of her children. In short, excessive reliance on alcohol led her from trauma to further trauma, which caused her to rely even more heavily on drinks. The end result of this dependence was death—the young woman died of liver failure. She had been called a survivor following her assault, but she ultimately did not survive.

SUBSTANCE USE AND ABUSE

Unfortunately, this woman's story is not unusual. Post-traumatic stress disorder and substance abuse disorders often go hand in hand.[1] When, like the pear tree, we are injured by trauma, our instinct is to get over or mask the pain as quickly as possible. Drugs and alcohol may seem like quick ways to mask that pain. The problem is, these artificial coping mechanisms do not lead to true healing. They are mere substitutes.

Alcohol and marijuana (in some states) are legal and easy to access, so these are commonly used to self-medicate. Drug abuse can also include using illegal street drugs, such as cocaine, heroin, and methamphetamines. While trauma survivors are at an increased risk of using these substances, many of us probably believe we would never be tempted to use illegal substances and wouldn't know where to obtain them.

Legally obtained opioids pose a much more devious threat. When a physician prescribes a painkiller, we tend to trust it's safe, but prescription opioids can be as addicting, mind-altering, and lethal as drugs obtained illegally. Many people who initially take these substances in good faith under the care of a physician fall prey to powerful addictions. Additionally, obtaining and using opioids without a doctor's supervision is highly problematic. While they provide effective temporary pain relief following an injury, surgery, or other physical trauma, opioids are not intended for long-term use—and, for good reason, they should never be used to numb emotional pain.

Friend, I want to caution you. Although drugs and alcohol may seem to offer temporary relief from suffering, they will not heal your trauma.

MEDICATION VERSUS SELF-MEDICATING

The substances we have discussed so far can alter your perceptions, behavior, coordination, and much more. But I am not suggesting that all medications should be avoided. Following trauma, the chemicals and hormones in our bodies that regulate our moods and emotions can be significantly altered. When these receptors change, we can experience severe depression and anxiety. There are times when medication is necessary to stabilize our emotions. This is fairly common following traumatic experiences. Medications that restore and balance our receptors can be an essential part of the healing process, stabilizing us as we walk *through* trauma. I encourage you to seek the help of a physician if needed. Medical management for depression and anxiety is far different from self-medicating in an attempt to get *over* trauma.

I have often heard people say they will never take medications for mental wellness. Some fear that taking medications is an indicator that they are mentally ill. This is a stigma I would like to address.

Our bodies contain many chemicals and hormones that can become dysregulated. A person with diabetes is dealing with a chemical issue. Either his or her body is not producing insulin, or it is resistant to the insulin it produces. Insulin is a hormone, just like adrenaline, dopamine, and endorphins. The difference is that insulin is produced in the pancreas and the other hormones are found in the brain. If a person with diabetes refused to take medications and instead decided to "just try harder" to produce insulin, his or her diabetes would not be controlled. We are unable to produce insulin simply by trying harder.

The same is true for the hormones and chemicals found in our brains. If a person becomes clinically depressed or suffers from severe anxiety, "trying harder" will not fix the brain's receptors. The brain is no different from any other organ in the body. Sometimes it requires medicinal help. Your doctor can assist you in figuring out if medicine is necessary and what kind might be helpful.

> *If a person becomes clinically depressed or suffers from severe anxiety, "trying harder" will not fix the brain's receptors.*

I have heard others say they will not take antidepressants or antianxiety medicine because doing so shows a lack of faith in God. If you are someone who struggles to accept the need for medication, I challenge you to reframe your perspective. Please ask yourself, does taking medication to treat diabetes demonstrate a lack of faith? We have been "fearfully and wonderfully made" by a perfect God (Psalm 139:14). He knows the biology of our bodies because He created us. Can we praise God for giving us a little peek into the science of how He designed us, enabling medical professionals to treat our bodies when necessary?

If you need medicinal support during your recovery, please give yourself some grace. While no one should pressure you to take medication, it is okay to talk to your doctor about options to help you during this time. Make your decision based on valid research and your own values. This is much healthier than self-medicating with substances that are not regulated and can't heal you.

SUBSTITUTING RELATIONSHIPS

The use and abuse of substances is only one example of substitutions we employ to avoid walking through the healing process. When trauma involves the loss of relationship, as with divorce or the death of a partner, many people find themselves entering new relationships too quickly. There is a reason why mental health professionals advise against doing so. People and relationships are not replaceable. We cannot simply substitute one relationship for another.

On the surface this sounds like common sense, doesn't it? But remember that one of our needs, according to Maslow, is love and belonging. We instinctively try to fill that need when we lose a source of love and connection. But jumping into a relationship too quickly often leads to further trauma. Take time to heal first. If you choose to pursue a relationship in the future, having walked through the healing process will allow you to bring the best of yourself into that relationship.

SUICIDAL IDEATION

It's vital that I talk briefly here about suicidal ideation. Suicide is the exact opposite of survival. It is not a coping strategy; it is surrendering to pain that seems endless and hopeless. But, friend, while you may feel hopeless now, this moment will pass. So as impossible as things may seem, please don't give up. Remember that nothing is impossible with the help of God.

If you feel so hopeless that suicide begins to sound like a way out, please tell someone. Go to an emergency room or dial 988 to reach someone who can talk through these thoughts with you. Help is available when you feel hopeless.

Mental Health Crisis
and Suicide Prevention
Dial 988

AVOIDANCE AND DENIAL

Another way we substitute artificial coping for true healing is through denial and avoidance. Many of us try to pack traumatic memories away in a box and set it on a high shelf in the back of our minds. I did this following my assault. I decided life had been good the day before the attack, and I wasn't going to let one incident change that for me. So I returned to class the following Monday and threw myself back into my other activities. I avoided counseling because I didn't want to talk about what had happened. Discussing it with my friends and family would mean seeing their grief for me, and I wasn't prepared to face that.

Thirty-five years later, when I received the call that my cold case was being re-opened, I learned that storing trauma in a box in my brain was similar to storing old photographs. Although I didn't think about the memories, they were still there, and reopening my case also reopened that box. I experienced post-traumatic stress symptoms as if I were eighteen again and the incident had just happened.

Again, God didn't create us to get *over* trauma. He wants to walk with us as we work *through* it. Isaiah 43:2 says,

> When you pass *through* the waters,
> I will be with you;
> and when you pass *through* the rivers,
> they will not sweep over you.
> When you walk *through* the fire,
> you will not be burned;
> the flames will not set you ablaze.

How can this be? Because the Great Physician is there to heal. The Wonderful Counselor is there to comfort. The God of all creation will never leave your side, even as you walk *through* this storm.

AUTHENTIC HEALING

There is no substitute for the healing power of God. There is no substitute for the coping mechanisms He has given us for weathering the storms of life. I know moving beyond trauma is difficult, I truly do. But I also know that the beauty and joy that await you on the other side of this journey are far beyond the Franken-mess that comes from substitutions.

For Barry and me, grafting branches into our pear tree might have given the illusion that it was fuller and more alive, but it would have never made our tree whole again. In fact, those grafts would not have led to life, as the tree wouldn't have sustained grafts from different fruit trees. In the same way, jumping into a relationship too quickly or self-medicating or otherwise avoiding the processing of your trauma are grafts that will not lead to life. Though they promise they'll get you over the trauma to healing, they're destructive illusions.

While so far we've been setting up the context for healing, the rest of this book will offer you a practical map for the journey *through* the healing process. One step at a time. You have survived so far. Now let's figure out how to flourish.

Questions for Reflection

1. What substitutes have you used or thought about using when life was difficult?

2. Have you become dependent on an artificial coping strategy? Might you need help to break this dependency?

Even when I walk through the darkest valley,
I will not be afraid, for you are close beside me.
Your rod and your staff protect and comfort me.

PSALM 23:4 (NLT)

CHAPTER 7

Managing the Unmanageable

A woman I'll call "Chloe" had struggled with anxiety for as long as she could remember. But now, facing some truly busy and uncertain times, she was feeling especially overwhelmed.

She was just completing her bachelor of science degree and facing the daunting challenge of her state's licensing examination. Anxiety had always made test taking challenging, but the stakes seemed even higher now. Engaged to be married, Chloe imagined that everything depended on her passing the exam. Once she had her license, she and her fiancé could look for jobs to finance their wedding and future home. Chloe had not experienced trauma when I first met her, but she was facing the stress that many people experience during life transitions.

One day, Chloe, looking exhausted and stunned, shared that her best friend, a single mother, had passed away suddenly the week before, leaving behind her four-month-old son, "Trey." The father of the baby had moved out of the country and was not interested in returning for his child. As Chloe was struggling to process her shock and grief, her best friend's mother arrived at her house with Trey. She informed Chloe that it was her friend's wish that Chloe raise the baby. The grandmother left Trey in Chloe's care immediately. That same week, Chloe learned that she herself was pregnant.

Already burdened with anxiety, Chloe now also struggled with trauma and grief. She wanted to honor her friend's request but was overwhelmed. She felt she needed to pass her testing as soon as possible to pursue the career that would support her, Trey, and her expected child. Her fiancé, though supportive, still had a year of college to complete before he would begin his own career. The couple had jumped from the stress of completing school and planning a wedding to immediately parenting and providing for a family.

Grieving the sudden loss of her friend on its own would have been a lot for Chloe to handle. This went well beyond. Chloe would be required to participate in home visits, evaluations, and court hearings to gain guardianship of Trey—all while preparing to take her state exam. She would also need immediate housing arrangements to obtain guardianship.

Chloe wondered, "What do I do now?"

This is often our first question when we are overwhelmed, isn't it? But maybe it isn't the best question to start with.

Rather than trying to figure it all out in a day, we need to take a breath and figure out what needs to be done first. It's often helpful to begin with the question, "What should I *not* do?"

COMPARTMENTALIZING

Most traumatic events present a mix of complicated, multifaceted, and confusing challenges, sometimes during already stressful times. No single action will fix everything. The first step is triage.

We must begin by prioritizing which things need to happen immediately, and then we mentally create boxes for other things that can wait. This method is called *compartmentalizing*. I imagine putting all the tasks and decisions into various boxes, covering them with lids, and setting them aside for the time being. Choose only two priorities to address the first week.

Everything else can be stored away and dealt with later. Don't worry—those things will eventually be dealt with. Challenges don't go away when we store them; they simply wait their turn to receive our attention. Each week, you can review the chaos again and decide which boxes need to be opened that week. Everything else can wait.

PRUNING

Once we have compartmentalized, we begin to examine our boxes and repeat the triage process. As we decide which tasks need our attention, we may notice that some boxes are consistently saved for later. Over time, some of the boxes will become less stressful, and some will be deemed nonessential or unnecessary. This is the beginning of the pruning season. To prune means "to remove anything considered superfluous or undesirable."[1] The purpose of pruning a tree is to conserve its energy and make room for more fruitful growth. Pruning shapes the tree for maximum growth potential. We need to prune things back during chaotic times in life. This not only helps us survive but also helps us shape the outcomes for growth.

Most of us have much that could be pruned from our schedules. Prior to the death of her best friend, Chloe had been overwhelmed with school activities, exam preparation, graduation arrangements, and wedding plans. Now that she was caring for Trey and pregnant, she decided that planning a big wedding was no longer a priority. She spoke with her fiancé, and they adjusted their plans. They kept parts of the wedding that were important to them, but they chose a smaller ceremony with less planning, no DIY projects, and far fewer expenses. This is a great example of pruning.

As we continue the triage process, some boxes *will* prove to be essential. We can't prune the essentials. For example, Chloe couldn't prune her state exam. She needed to successfully complete it to pursue her career. We may find it necessary to rearrange our schedules or to utilize our support systems to address the essential boxes we have set aside.

What things might you be able to prune in your life? Are there relationships that sap you of energy? Maybe you are one who often takes care of others. Might this be a time to take a break and allow others to assist you in some way? During chaotic times, many people attempt to continue with activities they see as good and meaningful. But this may be a season when you need to rest from these activities. Later in this book, we will talk about the importance of moving beyond our pain and focusing on others. Right now, though, you may need to prune some busyness and caretaking from your schedule while you focus on caring for yourself.

BOUNDARIES

Once we compartmentalize and prune, we begin to work on setting and keeping good boundaries. One of the stressors Chloe faced was finding time for her parents as she dealt with her heavy load.

Chloe and her fiancé wanted to plan their wedding and find a home for their new, growing family, but she was distracted. She knew her parents were struggling to adjust to an empty nest. She wanted to make the transition easier by spending time with her family, but it was necessary to set boundaries. Setting boundaries can be difficult for many reasons. Most often, the boundary setter doesn't want to offend someone or wants to protect the feelings of someone. This was the case with Chloe. She felt that setting boundaries with her parents would be perceived as disrespectful.

Counselors Henry Cloud and John Townsend talk about boundaries as property lines.[2] I often use this analogy with people. When faced with a dilemma, first identify what problem is creating the disconnect, then figure out whose property it lives on. If the problem doesn't live on your property, it is not yours to fix. It is perfectly acceptable to prevent your neighbor's weeds from growing on your property. In Chloe's case, her parents' difficulty in facing an empty nest lived squarely on their property. Chloe could be sensitive to her parents' struggle, but she couldn't fix it for them. When we experience guilt in setting boundaries, it is often a sign that someone else's weeds are growing on our property.

> *If the problem doesn't live on your property, it is not yours to fix.*

Of course, often others don't like it when we set boundaries. When people respond to our boundaries with anger or sadness, we need to allow those emotions to live on their property. It is tempting to loosen our boundaries to make others feel better, but that isn't our job. For example, Chloe learned to allow the anger and sadness to live on her parents' property. She understood that they would also have to process *through* their emotions and that it was not her responsibility to help them get *over* the transition. This was a healthy move for both Chloe and her parents. Chloe did not take her parents' stress onto her own property, and her parents were able to begin processing their own emotions. Win-win.

BALANCE, GROWTH, AND STRENGTH

In this chapter we tackled how to manage what seems unmanageable. Compartmentalizing helps us prioritize and focus on one thing or a few important things at a time. Pruning removes unnecessary things that drain our energy. Boundary setting prevents us from taking on issues that are not ours to solve.

My little pear tree, with its two broken branches sticking out in opposite directions, had been *more* than adequately pruned. But while pruning can be painful, proper pruning creates balance, promotes growth, and strengthens the structure of a tree. You might feel like that wounded pear tree right now, but maybe these simple ways of removing needless tasks and stress will help you preserve energy, grow in strength, and find balance.

Questions for Reflection

1. Are there unhealthy relationships, unnecessary obligations, or other time wasters you can remove from your schedule?

2. What would it take to prune these things from your life?

Don't worry about tomorrow, for tomorrow will bring its own worries. Today's trouble is enough for today.

MATTHEW 6:34 (NLT)

PART II

Moving Through Trauma

CHAPTER 8

Mending the Wounds

I have mentioned post-traumatic stress disorder (PTSD) in earlier chapters. Can I be honest? I really do not like the term. The word *disorder* in PTSD implies that PTSD is something one is born with. It is not. I much prefer "post-traumatic stress *injury*" (PTSI). PTSI refers to the injury, or biological trauma, that affects the nervous system.

Changing the name to post-traumatic stress injury is not a new concept, nor is it my original idea. Many have been advocating for an official change for years.[1] When a mental health professional diagnoses a mental health issue, we use diagnostic criteria and codes similar to what physicians use when diagnosing an illness. The American Psychological Association (APA) publishes a book of the guidelines for diagnosis: the *Diagnostic and Statistical Manual of Mental Disorders* (DSM-5-TR). The latest updates to this manual were made in 2022, but the name *post-traumatic stress disorder* remains unchanged. While I will subsequently use PTSI in this book, I acknowledge that the APA still only recognizes PTSD as a diagnosis.

Why does any of this matter? Well, many perceive a *disorder* as an abnormal psychological or mental condition. *But the symptoms of PTSI are not abnormal.* Not at all. They are the brain's normal response to significant trauma. It would be abnormal to experience big "T" Trauma and *not* have any level of disturbance.

Our brains were created to protect us from danger. Think about it. A child who has no understanding of the word *hot* may choose to touch the pan even when a parent warns them. Once the child touches the hot pan, the brain stores that information in a new way. Henceforth the child will be more vigilant around hot things. He or she may have anxiety relating to being burned or have nightmares relating to heat. This is a normal, healthy response to experiencing something painful. The response is how we learn to make safe and rational decisions about our environment. God created us to react this way for a reason.

PTSI is the set of symptoms that occurs when our brains react to pain and suffering beyond the realm of normal. The symptoms of PTSI can include intrusive thoughts and flashbacks, sleep disturbances, increased anxiety, hypervigilance, nightmares, depression, mood changes, memory problems, and more. Unfortunately, PTSI can cause a person to partake in unhealthy behaviors, such as detaching from family and friends and avoiding essential situations that are reminiscent of the event; it can beget substance abuse and even suicide (as discussed in chapter 6). In short, PTSI is a normal response that can result in dysfunctional behavior. But treating the symptoms can prevent disordered behavior.

> *The response is how we learn to make safe and rational decisions about our environment. God created us to react this way for a reason.*

Post-traumatic stress symptoms occur because of an injury. Think of a broken bone. When someone breaks a leg, we don't instantly conclude that person was born with deficient bones. Rarely does a bone break because of a preexisting disorder. It breaks because of abnormal pressure or impact. We treat the injury.

There is much scientific evidence that PTSI is the result of an actual *physical* injury. In *The Body Keeps the Score*, Dr. Bessel van der Kolk shares how one's brain and body are both injured by trauma.[2] Untreated PTSI can lead to digestive issues, chronic pain, heart palpitations, and chronic fatigue. Neuropsychologists have discovered that parts of the brain are physically changed following trauma. Following a big "T" Trauma or chronic little "t" trauma, the amygdala—remember that little emotionally charged, irrational part of the brain?—grows. At the same time, the hippocampus, the rational part of the brain that tells the amygdala to calm down when danger is not imminent, shrinks. It is vitally important to acknowledge this change as an actual injury to respect the dignity of those who have suffered trauma. (It breaks my heart that the Pentagon still does not award the Purple Heart to those who suffer from PTSI but will award it for a ruptured eardrum. But I digress.)

Hear me: If you are struggling with PTSI, you are not disordered. You are not abnormal. You have experienced something that is beyond what your brain was meant to comprehend. But I have good news for you. Injuries can be healed. Wounds can be mended!

TREATING THE INJURY

Because mental health professionals have so much information on how the body and brain are impacted by trauma, providers have been able to develop interventions that can effectively treat injuries. We have already discussed the importance of meeting basic needs in the aftermath of trauma. These are the first steps toward healing, but we can go much further. Let's talk about some practical and therapeutic things you can do to help the healing process.

Proverbs is a book in the Bible that is brimming with wisdom. I love verse 22 of chapter 15: "Plans fail for lack of counsel, but with many advisers they succeed." That tells me we are not meant to figure out life alone. We have talked about the importance of including God in every step of our healing journey, but we need to let other human beings join the trip too. Just as I believe that God sometimes answers our prayers for physical healing by preparing and sending physicians to treat our bodies, I also believe God has prepared and sent therapists to help with our emotional healing. We don't have to navigate this alone.

MYTHS ABOUT THERAPY

Let's talk about some beliefs that might be holding you back from seeking help. Maybe you believe that therapy provided by a mental health professional is only for the severely mentally ill. In reality, therapy is also helpful for the average healthy, happy, hurting, grieving, confused, angry, kind, struggling, goal-oriented human being.

Did you hear that?

A doctor is not for the terminally ill only. A doctor helps folks who have been through physical trauma return to a healthy status. That is the role of a mental health professional as well. Every one of us could likely benefit from counseling at some point in our lives.

Unfortunately, myths about psychotherapy have arisen in Christian communities. Some believe that seeking therapy is not a biblically sound thing to do. Some say that therapy disregards the reality of sin and that mental health diagnoses are used as an excuse for bad behavior. Let me be clear. A diagnosis does not remove personal responsibility. Therapy, done well, will allow you to explore some of the whys of your behavior and emotions, but it will also encourage growth and responsibility so those behaviors aren't repeated and so emotions can be regulated.

Another myth about counseling argues that because God is one's strength, seeking help anyplace else is a sign of weakness. I understand where this idea comes from. Of course we want to rely on God for spiritual, physical, and emotional healing. But therapy is not a substitute for God. He often uses professionals to be His hands and feet here on earth.

Many of us erroneously believe we must have it all together to show others that

God is good. Friend, no one has it all together! In many Bible translations, there are over a hundred references to each of the following words: *heal, comfort, redeem, hope, restore* . . . and others. If Christians were expected to have it all together, God wouldn't have inspired the use of such words in the Bible. Experiencing negative emotions does not mean you are a disappointment to God. Even Jesus wept (John 11:35).

> *Experiencing negative emotions does not mean you are a disappointment to God.*

That said, once you've decided to go to therapy, it's important to find a therapist who is a good fit for you. Many of you might find that having a Christian therapist is important in helping you feel comfortable and free to share. If that's the case, don't be afraid to ask if your potential therapist is a Christian. And when you search, be sure to read each therapist's bio. Many of us will mention that we offer Christian counseling or work for Christian counseling centers. Your church will likely know of Christian counselors or therapists in your area and may even have someone on staff.

If you meet with a counselor and don't feel it is a good fit, you have every right to end that relationship and look elsewhere. Good therapists want you to find a fit that is comfortable for you, and some may even recommend another therapist in your area.

TYPES OF THERAPY

Take into consideration the type of therapy a therapist offers. There are many different approaches to trauma therapy. I will talk about only a few here, and I will tell you what I recommend.

Most approaches to the treatment of trauma use *talk therapy,* such as cognitive behavioral therapy (CBT), interpersonal therapy, and psychodynamic therapy. Each of these can be helpful in treating PTSI. In all of them, a therapist and client sit in a room together and talk through the trauma, as well as related emotions, thought processes, and coping strategies.

Talk therapy often uses exposure to address trauma. The idea is to expose someone to painful memories by talking about them until they become less painful to discuss. Some researchers have found this to be effective over time; however, it can be a long, difficult process. There is no timeline for how long, nor is there any magic number of how many times a person will need to revisit the trauma before he or she can talk about it without emotional disturbance.

CBT in particular may also help to change certain thinking patterns. For example, if trauma has instilled in a person an unrealistic pattern of fearing danger, therapy might center on reframing that person's thought patterns toward positive outcomes and self-confidence. Rather than having her mind absorbed by negative, catastrophic thinking, she would focus on understanding her trauma from a perspective of strength and on recognizing the skills and resources she has for coping.

While I believe talk therapy can be beneficial, I believe there is a more effective, efficient approach to treating PTSI. I recommend searching for a therapist who is trained in eye movement desensitization reprocessing (EMDR), which is uniquely designed to treat trauma where it lives. Let me explain.

I have mentioned a couple of times that the amygdala is the part of the brain that stores memories related to strong emotions. This nugget of information will help you to understand why EMDR is effective for trauma recovery. Remember, this little almond-sized piece of our brain is where trauma lives—but we can't simply open up the amygdala and make whatever adjustments we want by talking through our thoughts. When we have conversations, like we do in talk therapy, we use a completely different part of the brain. We can talk about our feelings without actually "feeling the feels." In fact, we can even talk about our feelings without mentioning feelings at all.

"How are you feeling?"

"Fine."

Fine is not an emotion. Neither are *okay, good,* or *perfect*. Although you have replied to someone's question about your feelings, you've simply given conversational answers. We needn't access true emotion to respond to the question.

Now, we could have that conversation and try to consciously identify what feelings we are experiencing in the moment, but it would still be conscious thought for the purpose of communication. That thought takes place in the prefrontal cortex of the brain. (You don't need to remember the names of the parts of the brain; you simply need to understand that the prefrontal cortex and amygdala have different purposes and are in different areas of the brain.)

Because traumatic memories and emotions live in the amygdala, we must access that part of the brain in order to mend the wounds of trauma. Since talk therapy alone focuses on the conscious brain, it is important to find a therapist who also uses techniques that target the emotional center of the trauma.

Think of it this way. I once injured my shoulder. I had torn cartilage and separated muscle from bone. At first, the surgeon I saw recommended ice and physical therapy—both excellent treatments. But still, while the ice reduced my pain and swelling, for months the only way to get a good night's sleep was to keep ice on my shoulder. And while physical therapy helped me maintain my existing range of motion, it didn't bring back the mobility I had prior to the injury. The only way to fix the cartilage and reattach the muscle was surgery. While I waited, ice and physical therapy helped me function daily. But the surgery was what restored my mobility, increased my strength, and cured my pain.

I have counseled clients for decades and was trained in EMDR just a few years ago. I have found EMDR to be a powerful tool for trauma survivors, doing the work of a surgeon and curing the actual injury.

Talk therapy is like ice. It soothes the pain, reduces the harm, and gets us by. It is a great treatment, and it's necessary *after* surgery as well as before. But to find healing from triggering thoughts, nightmares, hypervigilance, depression, panic attacks—all the things that live in the amygdala—we need more.

EMDR THERAPY

I want to demystify the most misunderstood component of EMDR therapy. The *eye movement* of *eye movement desensitization reprocessing* originated because of a theory that moving our eyes back and forth would help process thought on a subconscious level. When we sleep deeply, our mind processes the events of our day. We call this deep sleep REM (rapid eye movement) sleep.

Some Christians have inaccurately linked these eye movements to hypnosis. This is why some are fearful of EMDR. I want to be clear—if your EMDR therapist asks you to watch a light move back and forth or to follow their fingers with your eyes, they are not using hypnosis. They are using bilateral stimulation, which allows a trauma survivor to process difficult memories while simultaneously being reminded that this is now and she is in a safe place.

Eye movements are only one way to create bilateral stimulation. *Bilateral* simply means both sides of the brain are included. Other methods of bilateral stimulation are also effective for EMDR therapy. Rather than engaging in eye movement, you may be asked to hold two little devices that vibrate back and forth between your left and right hands, or you may wear headphones that alternate beeps between ears. Some therapists have you tap your own shoulders one after the other. Bilateral stimulation can be very comforting and grounding as you process traumatic memories.

The rest of EMDR is simply reprocessing the emotions and negative thoughts associated with your trauma so you are not easily triggered in the future. It is amazing how capable our brains are of healing themselves with the right guidance.

AN EMDR CASE STUDY

"Gabrielle" had suffered ongoing big "T" Trauma throughout her childhood and into her early adult years. She had been in counseling for several years, and her complex PTSI was complicated to treat.

Gabrielle was a bright woman with a perpetual smile. Her intelligence was evident, and she seemed to exude confidence. With a smile on her face, she told about being physically and sexually abused by her stepfather and his father from the age of four until she was twelve years old.

I was struck by Gabrielle's lack of emotion as she shared her story, but I soon learned that her smile was her defense system. She had always felt that if she stayed sweet, maybe she could avoid the harsh physical abuse her stepfather wielded. She had become a people pleaser as a form of self-preservation.

Gabrielle participated in EMDR therapy weekly. As she processed old memories, she had difficulty connecting with her past emotions. She would tell stories while remaining emotionally detached throughout. She had dissociated and could describe events as if they were scenes from an old movie.

Gabrielle was asked to picture herself as a young child, and then to imagine her adult self sitting with her younger self during one of those difficult times. Gabrielle was able to imagine things she would say to that child. She viewed the little girl as separate from herself, but she knew what the little girl needed to hear. She imagined telling her younger self that she didn't deserve the abuse and that she was going to grow up one day and things would be different. She proceeded to tell her younger self that one day she would be a mom and that she would grow up to protect her children.

Gabrielle didn't need to verbalize these thoughts. She simply imagined the conversations playing out as she held on to bilateral stimulation tappers to remind her, *I am here* and *this is now*.

After a few sessions of processing this way, Gabrielle wanted to merge her younger self with her grown self. But she needed to wait a bit longer because, while she was able to imagine telling the little girl that she was loved and precious, she needed to acknowledge that she and the little girl were both the same person. Gabrielle processed until she was able to accept that her adult self was also loved and precious. Once she made that connection, she was able to imagine her younger self and her adult self merging into one loved, redeemed human being.

Gabrielle then began to weep openly. She acknowledged her pain and loss, but she also accepted that she deserved to be loved and respected. She was exhausted at the end of the session, but she said she had never felt so complete in her entire life. She was whole, and wholly worthy of so much better.

This is just one example of someone who benefited from EMDR therapy. Each person is different, and the process varies broadly, but it thrills me how often I hear people share that EMDR therapy has changed their perspective on life in profound ways.

Most importantly, after reprocessing traumatic memories with more rational emotions, many people have been delivered from the triggers and symptoms of PTSI. Once we begin to believe we are worthy and capable, we thwart the amygdala's hijacking of our emotions. Memories related to trauma cause far less disturbance, and the symptoms of PTSI resolve.

I encourage you to search for a therapist to join you on your journey to healing. Again, during your search, consider who will be a good match for you. Most agencies and practices today have a website that includes bios of each therapist. The bio will give you an idea of what to expect. Most will mention EMDR or faith-based counseling in the bio if this is something they offer. If not, call various practices in your area and ask the questions that are important to you in finding a good fit. Finding a therapist you feel comfortable with is the first and most important step in getting the help you seek.

Questions for Reflection

1. If you do not yet have a therapist, what next step are you willing to take toward finding one?

2. What therapeutic strategy or strategies stand out to you as something you might like to try?

He heals the brokenhearted and binds up their wounds.

PSALM 147:3

CHAPTER 9

Cultivating the Healing Process at Home

*P*sychotherapy, sometimes combined with medication, is the therapeutic equivalent of having surgery to repair a wound. After the operation, much healing must occur at home. Likewise, as you progress through therapy, you will find there are things you can do on your own to help the healing process along. In this chapter, we will talk about self-help that can be used to supplement therapeutic interventions. Notice I used the word *supplement* here. These techniques are not meant to replace the help you will find with a mental health professional.

In many cases, a therapist will schedule you for weekly or biweekly appointments. During those appointments, you will focus intently on processing your trauma experience. When you leave the therapist's office, it's not as if your mind will simply stop processing until your next appointment. I want to share some ideas for continuing to process daily in order to achieve healthy results.

JOURNALING

One of the greatest tools for processing thoughts and emotions is journaling. Following trauma, many people lie awake at night with questions, worries, regrets, and fears all fighting for space in brains that simply need rest. Journaling is a great way to capture our racing thoughts so we can more easily process, organize, and prioritize the chaos in our minds.

Our brains can produce thoughts much faster than we can write. Journaling helps us slow down and focus on one thing at a time. The practice can bring clarification to overwhelming thoughts. Often, once we write something down, we can then set that thing aside, knowing it will still be there to work on at another time.

> *Journaling helps us slow down and focus on one thing at a time.*

I recommend journaling with this caveat: Journaling can go sideways if we focus only on the pain and sorrow of our situations. Don't get me wrong. Healing doesn't mean you need to forget the pain of what happened. But it is about giving pain a place to go so happy memories have space to breathe. A journal is a great way to acknowledge pain and give it a place to live rather than allowing it to take over the soul. You will most definitely write about pain and sorrow, but don't stop there. I encourage you to journal with purpose and direction. Let me explain.

When my big "T" Trauma occurred, I wrote all the ugly details down in a notebook, then hid the words away in my nightstand, where the notebook lived for thirty-five years. The painful words I had written never changed; they simply marinated in the misery from which they were written. Then one day I decided to purge all things that reminded me of negative life events. I threw away divorce papers and reminders of darker times in life. For the most part, this was a healthy pruning. As I was pruning, I remembered that notebook in my nightstand. I pulled the notebook out of my nightstand and tore the pages up. I said out loud, "God, I am done with this. It's Yours." The only problem was, I wasn't really done. I hadn't processed the trauma contained on those pages.

It was only a week later that I learned my perpetrator had been identified. I don't think it was a coincidence that my case was reopened only after I gave it to God. He didn't bring justice as I had hoped, but He used this time to reveal my unhealed wounds. I had to let go of the preserved, painful words before He began His work in me. When I received the news that my cold case would be reopened, it wasn't as if the pain had gone away. I crumbled. I questioned why God would choose to hand the trauma right back to me. What was He thinking?

Shortly after, I decided to begin journaling again. Because life seemed upside-down and inside-out, I figured it might be cathartic to journal with white ink on black paper. (That is just how my creative mind works, I guess.) The first thing I wrote on those black pages was the same verse I mentioned in the introduction, Psalm 27:13. I was sure it was promising I would get the two things I wanted most—justice and closure. In my mind, those concepts represented the goodness of the Lord, and I was confident both would happen in my lifetime.

I started my journal by literally returning to the scene of the crime and sitting under the window of the room where it happened. All day I wrote about my anger, brokenness, fear, anxiety, fury, sorrow, and despair. The ugliness of my trauma glared in white ink on black paper.

When I finished writing, I felt pretty miserable. I had questions and I wanted answers. I decided to look through what I had written, and I noticed that certain themes stood out. Mostly I had written about justice and anger. So I searched the internet for what Scripture had to say on justice. Of the many verses that popped up, two spoke to me, and I wrote them down. Then I did the same thing for anger.

I was still struggling, but writing the verses allowed me to give God space to speak into my journal.

I continued this practice for an entire year. Every day I started by writing raw—the good, the bad, and the ugly—there in white ink on black paper. I ended each session by looking for themes, searching for Scripture on the ones that emerged, and writing down one or two verses that stood out to me.

At the end of that year, I was astounded by what had happened. My journal had become a dialogue with God. I would rage and He would soothe. I would cry and He would comfort. I would question and He would answer. Journaling had become a consistent and reliable conversation, the single most impactful conversation I have ever had. Together, God and I had written a bright future onto those dark pages.

I now encourage my clients to "Write R.A.W." It is a simple process.

R = **Raw Writing:** Pour your heart out. Write about your pain and what you are in the midst of dealing with.

A = **Ascertain the Themes:** Read back through what you have written and look for themes in your thoughts and emotions.

W = **Words from God:** Use a search engine and enter "Scripture about [theme]." Write down any verses that seem to speak to your situation.[1]

I understand that not everyone likes to journal. As I said, it can certainly go sideways into pain and sorrow if you don't make sure to find purpose and direction after the fact. But I encourage you to use this technique. Writing R.A.W. can be life-changing.

STRESS RESPONSE

In the last chapter, I mentioned that trauma can lead to physical challenges such as digestive issues, heart palpitations, and more. Because we know that trauma causes stress and stress impacts our bodies, it is important to discuss how to manage stress in healthy ways.

First, we need to pay attention to our bodies. Scripture says we are fearfully and wonderfully made. I love that those words remind us of how God made us with intention. God created our bodies and minds to work intricately together. It is impossible to take care of our bodies without engaging our minds. We must give thought to the food we eat, sleep schedules, exercise routines, and safety if we want to maintain a healthy body. The reverse is also true: To take care of our minds, we need to involve our bodies.

God created every living being with defense mechanisms to help us survive. A skunk protects itself with its repulsive spray. A porcupine's quills hook themselves deeply and painfully into the flesh of predators. But what is the human defense system? It is called the *stress response*. While it isn't quite as exotic as smelly spray or sharp quills, our stress response prepares us for fight or flight.

> *It is impossible to take care of our bodies without engaging our minds. The reverse is also true: To take care of our minds, we need to involve our bodies.*

Imagine you are walking along a quiet street when suddenly a huge, hungry tiger jumps out from behind a tree. Okay, that isn't likely, but it would definitely cause stress, right? Your body immediately begins to produce sweat to cool itself, preparing you for either physical combat or running. For a more ordinary scenario, have you ever simply gotten nervous and then felt shaky? That's because adrenaline was coursing through your system to supply strength and energy. In such situations, your heart rate increases and you begin to breathe heavily, increasing the oxygen sent to your limbs.

Whether we are facing a dangerous predator or feeling anxious about an uncertain future, our reaction to stress is the same. It's all our bodies' preparation to either fight threats or flee from them. But that fight-or-flight response—rapid heart rate, increased oxygen, adrenaline, and other physical changes—becomes problematic when we don't actually have to run or physically fight. Where then does all that oxygen and energy go? Our bodies become ill when we have a high level of stress response and no way to release it.

There are several strategies I'd recommend to manage your stress response. Each strategy falls into one of two categories: exercise or relaxation. These sound like opposites, don't they? But they have the same effect of calming our body's stress response. We can either use up the excess energy by exercising or stop producing the energy by relaxing. I will briefly mention exercise, but most of the strategies I'll discuss will focus on other types of relaxation techniques.

EXERCISE

After trauma, we tend to isolate ourselves. Depression can cause us to want to curl up on the couch and into ourselves to avoid further harm. Do just the opposite: Get up daily and move. You may not feel like going to a gym and being surrounded by people. That's okay. Go for a gentle walk, work in your garden, stretch . . . do what you can. The important thing is, *move*. The more active you become, the more adrenaline your body will release and the more oxygen you will expend. Walking in particular is a great time to focus on breathing and to talk with God about what is on your mind.

RELAXATION TECHNIQUES

Relaxation techniques can effectively calm your body and reduce its stress response. In the sections following, I share three of them: sensory vacations, progressive muscle relaxation, and listening to music. *Pay close attention to what you are feeling in your body* as you practice these techniques. We often say we feel stressed, but we don't really define *where* in our body we feel stress or *what* it feels like.

As you heal your trauma, I recommend that you practice these techniques every day, maybe even multiple times a day for a while.

Sensory Vacations

Since this first technique can be done in sixty seconds, it is sometimes called a *one-minute vacation*. I call it a *sensory vacation* because I don't like to limit it to a minute, and because involving all five of our senses is essential. A sensory vacation is a practical tool for combating stress throughout the day.

Begin by thinking of the most relaxing place you could possibly imagine. This could be a beach, a mountaintop, even a cloud made of cotton candy. The place can be real or imagined—just define what it is in your mind. Think of a name or a word to associate with that place. For example, I love to imagine myself lying on a sandy beach on Lake Michigan. The word I associate with that place is *waves*. You choose your own location and word.

Next, take a deep, cleansing breath in through your nose and out through your mouth. Imagine you are breathing in only the relaxed air molecules in the room and breathing out the stressed air molecules in your body. Breathe in relaxation, breathe out stress. Focus on relaxing your body so you feel like a deflated balloon at the end of the breath. Think of this cleansing breath as your transport to your relaxing destination.

As you finish your deep, cleansing breath, say the word aloud that represents your relaxing place, and imagine yourself in that place while breathing deeply and slowly.

Now imagine your surroundings using one sense at a time. Begin with sight: What do you see? Envision all the sights in that location; picture it all in your mind. Focus on seeing for at least ten seconds—but don't get distracted by trying to time yourself. Just enjoy the view.

Next, do the same for each of your other senses. What do you hear? What do you smell? What can you taste? What do you feel? Give your imagination free rein.

After you have walked through all your senses, scan your body and see what you notice. Do your muscles feel relaxed? If so, you might feel heavy. Go ahead and imagine that gravity is pulling you deeper into your soft surroundings. You might feel warmth or tingling. This is what it feels like as endorphins are released into your body. Endorphins are hormones that reduce stress, relieve pain, and improve mood. Deep breathing and sensory work can increase endorphins. What else do you notice? Pay close attention to what it *feels* like to relax and linger in that relaxation long enough to memorize the feeling.

Finally, when you are ready, take another deep, cleansing breath and open your eyes. That's it. You have completed your sensory vacation. Welcome back.

Involving your senses in this way tricks your brain. The brain will begin to produce fewer stress hormones such as cortisol and a greater number of calming receptors such as dopamine and serotonin. The sensations you'll feel in your body are a result of those changes. See what I mean? We are fearfully and wonderfully made!

I know it is a tough assignment, but take a vacation at least once each day. Allow God to wash his grace, healing, and comfort over you. After a while, you will notice that you can feel the signs of relaxation more quickly and sustain that comfortable state longer.

Progressive Muscle Relaxation

Once you have familiarized yourself with the sensory vacation, try adding progressive muscle relaxation (PMR) to your routine. This technique takes longer and requires that you sit or lie in a comfortable position. Many people find that bedtime is a great time to do PMR. Some express concern because they fall asleep before finishing this activity. To this I say, congratulations! If you fall asleep before completing the circuit, that's a very good sign that it's doing what it needs to do.

PMR helps you to recognize muscle tension in your body and what it feels like to relax that tension. This is done by systematically tensing muscle groups in your body and then slowly relaxing those muscles. Again, practice will make this process more efficient over time.

You will get the best results from PMR if you dress in comfortable clothes and find a quiet place where you can lie down or recline in a comfortable position. You will want to set aside at least twenty minutes for each session. Once you are comfortable, take a deep, cleansing breath, like you did for the sensory vacation, and close your eyes.

Begin at the top of your head and work toward your toes. I will propose a sequence here, but you may find ways to add other muscle groups as you practice. Remember to breathe deeply and slowly as you work through this process.

1. Squeeze the muscles of your forehead together as tightly as possible for fifteen seconds. Focus on what that tension feels like. Now slowly let those muscles relax. Breathe as you notice what that feels like. Do you feel warmth, tingling, or heaviness? Relax and pay attention to those muscles for about thirty seconds.

2. Squeeze your eyes tightly shut for fifteen seconds and, as in step 1, focus on feeling the tension in those muscles. Now relax your eye muscles and focus on what the relaxation feels like for thirty seconds. *Repeat this process for each of the next steps.*

3. Clench your teeth and force a large, uncomfortable smile. Pay attention to the muscles in your jaw.

4. Shrug your shoulders and tense your neck.

5. Pull your shoulder blades back and close together to tighten the muscles in your upper back.

6. Suck your stomach muscles in to feel tension in your torso.

7. Squeeze your buttocks together to feel tension in your hips and lower torso.

8. Lift one arm and make a fist. Pay attention to the tense muscles in your upper arm, forearm, wrist, hand, and fingers. Repeat with the other arm.

9. Lift one leg and point or flex your toes. Pay attention to the muscles in your hip, thigh, calf, ankle, foot, and toes. Repeat with the other leg.

Again, as you work through this process, spend fifteen seconds tensing each muscle group and at least thirty seconds relaxing and noticing the difference. For example, as you relax each arm and leg, you will notice that they feel heavier. Your shoulders should feel as if gravity is pulling them downward. Continue to pay close attention to what you feel.

I have given you a quick script to practice PMR on your own, but you may also want to look into online resources. You may enjoy listening to someone talk you through the process of relaxing your muscles. Some recordings include soft music, which can assist the healing process. I'll discuss this further in just a moment.

If you make it through the PMR process without falling asleep, you can simply enjoy the relaxation for as long as you wish, or you might want to take the opportunity to begin a sensory vacation. Combining PMR and sensory imagination work allows your body and brain to work together toward relieving stress. Again, practice both techniques frequently. You will notice over time that a deep, cleansing breath alone will signal your body to start producing those feel-good hormones and chemicals. You can train your body to de-stress more quickly and efficiently.

Music

I mentioned that music can be beneficial during relaxation. Let's talk about why. You'll recall that trauma lives in the amygdala, that tiny part of our brain that stores memory associated with strong emotion. Because the amygdala is an emotional component rather than a rational one, it can be tricky to access through cognition alone. EMDR is a recent method for involving the amygdala in emotional processing. But music has been doing this since the beginning of time.

The amygdala doesn't store only negatively charged memories; it stores subconscious memories linked with *all* strong emotions.

One Easter years ago, my brother and I were sitting in church with our respective kids. Earlier that week, he and I had watched a hilarious video of people singing in church—too loudly, off-key, or just plain badly. I don't remember what made that video so funny, but it found a place to live in our amygdalae. So that Easter morning, when the man behind us began singing really loudly . . . and then when he finished a song by shouting "Praise the LOOUURRD!" . . . uh-oh! He pulled our laugh triggers from that video.

Have you ever experienced a case of the giggles that just would not stop? My brother and I tried to stifle our laughter, but it spilled out of us until the tears ran down our faces. Our kids were mortified, but their disapproval just made us laugh all the harder. *Embarrassing* doesn't begin to describe it. We had to step out to pull ourselves together. That, my friend, is the work of the amygdala. It overflowed our systems with laughter, and we could not gain control.

The amygdala responds to music in a powerful way. Music can draw emotion out of us. Sometimes it makes us happy, sometimes sad. Movies use music to intentionally create an emotional response. What we listen to can have a great impact, positive or negative, on our emotional processing. What we listen to matters.

There's a Christian organization I'm fond of called Music for the Soul. Its founder and director, Steve Siler, used to write music for well-known Christian artists in Nashville. He founded the organization when he discovered the healing power music could have. The mission of Music for the Soul is to "work in partnership with donors, therapists, pastors, and those in recovery to create healing songs and stories that reflect the redemptive love of Jesus to those in deep pain."[2]

> *What we listen to can have a great impact on our emotional processing. What we listen to matters.*

I love that Steve was inspired to pull mental health professionals, pastors, musicians, and trauma warriors together to create a powerful tool for healing in the form of music. The organization also has a podcast I recommend. If you visit www.musicforthesoul.org, you can click on a topic that is meaningful to you and find healing music that will touch your heart.

Because I believe strongly in the healing power of music, I have also put together a playlist that can be found on my website, www.lisasaruga.com. The list is meant to offer hope and comfort. Many of the songs helped me in my own healing process. You might also want to put together your own playlist, or make several based on your varying needs. For example, a playlist of upbeat, happy music can be a mood changer. A playlist of worship songs can focus our attention on the majesty and power of God. Or maybe you want a playlist of soft, soothing instrumental music for times when you just want to relax. Give it a try. You may be surprised at how powerful music can be.

I pray that some of the activities in this chapter will bring you comfort and encouragement. And I hope you have a therapist who will share other ideas with you as well. May God bring you closer to Him and closer to healing with each step you take.

Questions for Reflection

1. What helps you to relax when you are stressed?

2. What songs have been encouraging to you?

Peace I leave with you; my peace I give to you.
Not as the world gives do I give to you. Let not your hearts
be troubled, neither let them be afraid.

JOHN 14:27 (ESV)

CHAPTER 10

Finding Hope

*M*iracle of miracles, our little pear tree survived the injury and went on to survive the winter! The following spring we noticed new growth—not just leaves but branches! The tree seemed to reach toward the sky and soak in the sunshine, trusting the light would bring healing and new life to each limb.

This is what hope looks like. It looks ahead to what is possible and stretches its arms toward the future. Hope is what gives us the ability to continue to put one foot in front of the other, even on days when the future seems like a scary, dark abyss we would rather avoid.

BEFORE AND AFTER

Following trauma, it is so difficult to imagine the future. When big "T" Trauma occurs, life often seems split into two categories: before and after. *Before* is the territory that is familiar and comfortable. I know many of us wish we could remain in the before, because we feel Big "T" Trauma has stolen something from us, but the truth is, there is no going back.

You may feel that the very thing stolen in the trauma *was* your hope for the future. I believe Larry and Dawn, whose story you read in chapter 2, felt this way about losing their children. Those of us who are parents frequently set our hopes on our children. We look forward to what they will accomplish in life, and we anticipate how our relationships with our kids as they grow up and maybe have children of their own will look. Every vision of our future is cross-pollinated with images of how our children will be involved, benefited, and shaped. Our kids season our hopes for the future and make our dreams seem even more delicious.

For parents, even dreams of a new home are filtered through the lens of our children. We envision where our children will sleep and play. We look for property that will create beautiful memories for them. But with the loss of children, that dream becomes tainted and damaged. How could we possibly continue to hope for a future home when the picture has changed so drastically?

DREAMS VERSUS HOPE

If your future dreams have been tainted by trauma, please do not be afraid to cling to hope. Hopes and dreams are not the same thing. Dreams are aspirations and ambitions that we turn into pictures of what life could be. Life can change our dreams over time. But hope! Hope is what changes life.

One definition of hope is "to look forward to with desire and reasonable confidence."[1] I love how this definition plays into that psalm of confidence and lament, Psalm 27, mentioned a few times in this book. Hope is a frame of mind that steadfastly holds on to confidence and trust. But confidence in what? Trust in whom? Let me remind you of verse 13:

> I remain confident of this:
>> I will see the goodness of the Lord
>> in the land of the living.

David, who wrote those words in Psalm 27, was no stranger to trauma. His life was in danger on many occasions: When he faced the giant Goliath. When the insane

King Saul was determined to kill him. When Absalom, his own son, challenged his kingship. David lost his best friend and his good reputation. Four of his children died. He was a man of high social status who lost everything, including the armies of men he had commanded. David suffered from depression and even talked at length of his suicidal thoughts. While many people find comfort in reading David's psalms of hope, I suspect David himself was very uncomfortable when he penned them. He wasn't exactly experiencing joy or readily seeing the goodness of the Lord. He was suffering.

Yet in Psalm 27:13 he clearly stated what he was confident of and whom he trusted. David expected to see goodness again in his lifetime. Earlier, David had been crying out to God about all the distress he was experiencing, but he persisted in his hope that he would see better days. More importantly, he placed his trust in God. As David wailed and grieved, he interrupted himself to say that God is good and powerful and trustworthy.

Notice how David tells God of his worries in Psalm 27:8–10 but alternates his fears with promises from God.

> You have said, "Look for My face." My heart said to You, "O Lord, Your face will I look for. Do not hide Your face from me. Do not turn Your servant away in anger. You have been my Helper. Do not turn away from me or leave me alone, O God Who saves me! For my father and my mother have left me. But the Lord will take care of me. (NLV)

Trusting in those promises is what gave David the strength to carry on in the face of difficult times. Likewise, trusting God's promises will strengthen us and give us hope. It might not feel natural to acknowledge God's goodness when nothing around us seems good, but you'll find power in interrupting your painful thoughts with reminders of God's promises.

MANTRAS OF GOD'S GOODNESS

Mantras of hope and trust in God are repeated many times throughout the book of Psalms, often by David himself. The psalmists seemed to understand that they had to force themselves to focus on a hopeful future that only God could foresee or provide because they didn't have it in themselves to find peace. The psalmists didn't give up on God, even when God seemed silent and uninvolved. Take a look at some of their statements.

> For you, LORD, have delivered me from death,
>   my eyes from tears,
>   my feet from stumbling,
> that I may walk before the LORD
>   in the land of the living.
>
> (Psalm 116:8–9)

> I cry to you, LORD;
>   I say, "You are my refuge,
>   my portion in the land of the living."
>
> (Psalm 142:5)

Ever notice that you can talk yourself into positivity or negativity? Sometimes we can let a negative statement or a false expectation form who we are. This occurrence is called a self-fulfilling prophecy. For example, if a child is told by parents, teachers, or other authority figures that he will never be successful and he believes that negative input, he is unlikely to strive for success.

Positive self-talk can do just the opposite. If we continuously tell ourselves that we are valuable, we will feel more valued. The psalmists were using positive God-talk. They repeatedly mentioned times when God had helped them in powerful ways. They frequently wrote that they knew God would save them, even when circumstances didn't look favorable. In essence, the psalmists were saying, "Even though I see no way forward, I trust you, God. I know you have good things planned, even if I can't see any path that could lead to safety, peace, or joy. I know you won't let me down, because you are ultimately good!"

We need to remind ourselves of God's power and goodness, especially when doubt wants to steal our hope. If you are unsure of where to begin, I hope you will find comfort in repeating the following verses to yourself.

> The LORD, the LORD, the compassionate and gracious God, slow
> to anger, abounding in love and faithfulness. (Exodus 34:6)

> The LORD loves righteousness and justice;
>   the earth is full of his unfailing love.
>   (Psalm 33:5)

> Do not fear, for I am with you;
>   do not be dismayed, for I am your God.
> I will strengthen you and help you;
>   I will uphold you with my righteous right hand.
>   (Isaiah 41:10)

> You will keep in perfect peace
>   those whose minds are steadfast,
>   because they trust in you.
>   (Isaiah 26:3)

> The LORD himself goes before you and will be with you; he
> will never leave you nor forsake you. Do not be afraid; do not
> be discouraged. (Deuteronomy 31:8)

> I will instruct you and teach you in the way you should go;
>   I will counsel you with my loving eye on you.
>   (Psalm 32:8)

Come to me, all you who are weary and burdened, and I will give you rest. Take my yoke upon you and learn from me, for I am gentle and humble in heart, and you will find rest for your souls. (Matthew 11:28–29)

Those who hope in the LORD
    will renew their strength.
They will soar on wings like eagles;
    they will run and not grow weary,
    they will walk and not be faint.
               (Isaiah 40:31)

My God will meet all your needs according to the riches of his glory in Christ Jesus. (Philippians 4:19)

GOD IS GOOD

My younger brother demonstrated unshakable hope in the face of a big "T" Trauma. He believed that God was good regardless of the outcome. He often reminded those around him that God was in control, because when he did so, he himself remembered. That is the power of a mantra. It is a constant reminder to others, and to ourselves, that hope lives.

At the age of thirty-three, Andy was diagnosed with pulmonary fibrosis. His prognosis was not good. The progressive lung scarring would lead to death in three to five years unless he could successfully obtain a double lung transplant. Andy and his wife had three small children and so many dreams for their future, but within a short period of time, he was forced to leave his career. As medical costs increased, the family lost their financial security and even their home. His condition continued to worsen, and the waiting list for transplant was long.

Andy was eventually dependent on an oxygen tank and, lacking the energy to walk, was often confined to a wheelchair. By the time my brother was thirty-seven, he looked like an old man. I confess I had begun to lose hope that he would live to see his children grow up. One night I asked him if he was afraid, because honestly, I was. My brother shocked me with his answer.

"The way I see it," he said, "this will go one of two ways. Either I will have a transplant and one day be able to play ball with my kids in our front yard, or I won't, and I will meet Jesus face-to-face. I can't lose."

Andy could have said he was afraid for his family or discouraged by the prognosis. He could have grieved the loss of his home, job, youth, and health. Actually, I am sure he did experience grieving all of those losses, but his mantra—"I can't lose"— showed that he trusted in the fact that God is good and God's goodness will never change. Talk about hope!

REAL HOPE

I want to be clear that hope is not the same thing as wishful thinking. Hope is rational; wishful thinking is irrational. Dawn and Larry's children were not returned to life. My perpetrator was never arrested. Chloe's friend did not return to raise her baby. The destruction of Japan's 2011 tsunami could not be undone. And Andy's lungs were not miraculously healed (though, as you will see, his story doesn't end there).

It would be wishful thinking to believe life could return to *before* when living in the *after* of trauma. Although God can and sometimes does work miracles, a more realistic hope is that we will experience goodness, peace, and even joy in the after regardless of miracles. Hope isn't dependent on miraculous healing, justice, or the undoing of what has already been done. We would be foolish to hang our hope on these things. Hope can only be found in something that is sure, true, and unchanging.

I have heard people say they lost faith in God because He allowed a trauma to occur. I understand. You have been hurt. You are sad, scared, grieving, and living with pain that it seems no one could possibly understand. It makes sense that you would question God in these times.

> *Hope can only be found in something that is sure, true, and unchanging.*

Why would You allow this to happen, God?

How could You have failed me in this?

Where are You, God?

The world may seem upside-down and inside-out for you in this season. Let me assure you of one thing: No one understands trauma better than Jesus.

Jesus came to this world fully human and fully God. He had the power to live a life untouched by trauma, but He didn't employ that power. Jesus knows exactly what it feels like to be a refugee with no safe place to call home. He knows what it feels like to lose a loved one, to be victimized by the rumor mill, to be beaten, to have His life threatened, to be betrayed by a close friend, to be robbed of everything He had, and to face an excruciating, torturous death. And God knows what it feels like to watch His child die. Even Jesus was not spared from trauma.

Scripture is clear that this life will bring both joy and suffering to each of us. We live in an imperfect, incomplete, unknowable world. In John 16:33, Jesus says, "I have told you these things, so that in me you may have peace. In this world you will have trouble. But take heart! I have overcome the world."

If Jesus had overcome the world, why did He suffer trauma? Because He was a human being living in a fallen and imperfect world. He wanted us to know that He understands, and because He understands, we can ask hard questions. Question away. Cry out in anger. Acknowledge your pain, just like David did in the Psalms. But also take heart.

What does it look like to "take heart"? How do you grab hold of this thing called hope?

BE HONEST WITH YOURSELF AND GOD

Start by acknowledging where you are right now. Acknowledge your pain, your loss, your confusion, your anger . . . all of it. Don't be afraid to ask God your hard questions. He is strong enough to handle your outrage and to love you anyway.

I am thinking of God as our Father. As a parent, I would never intentionally cause harm to my children. I would never dream of making one of my children sick to teach a lesson. My children are precious blessings to me, and I want nothing but the best for them. And I am a mere human being, imperfect in every way! God is the perfect Father to all His children. He loves us unconditionally and with perfection because He *is* love. God would never use trauma against you to punish you or to break you.

As much as I cherish my children, they have still been hurt, scared, sad, and even harmed. When my oldest son was two years old, he was excited about potty training. When he would announce that he needed to use the bathroom, we began a laborious process of encouraging, cheering, and celebrating. Following one of his announcements, I trotted behind him saying, "Good job. Let's get to the potty. Wow, you are incredible!" In his excited, joyous rush, he ran for the bathroom, but his little feet caught the lip of tile that marked the threshold to the bathroom. He tripped over the tile and hit the toilet face-first, breaking his little nose instantly.

What had begun as a potty party with the expectation of a post-potty celebration ended in a trip to the hospital with a sobbing, broken little boy. I still remember holding his hand and telling him how brave he was. After his hospital visit, I rocked him for as long as he wanted to rock and whispered how much I loved him and how proud I was of him. I held him close and felt his pain as if his body were my own. I would have done anything to make him feel better, so I poured my love into him in every possible way. I put my lips on his head and said, "I love you, Buddy. You are so brave. It's going to be okay. I promise you will feel better. I love you. Mommy will make sure you get all better. You are going to be okay."

Although I'd never wish a broken nose on my little boy, his recovery time stands out in my mind as a time of love, snuggles, comfort, reassurance, and powerful connection. It would break my heart if my son remembered it as a time when I tried to teach him to use the toilet by breaking his nose, and that he no longer loved or trusted me because of the event. Can you imagine? If he had rejected me because of his trauma, I'd have been powerless to comfort him and shower him with my love.

Now think about God. Would He, your heavenly Father, want to cause you pain? No, He wouldn't. Child, your Father didn't cause your pain. He was not trying to teach you a lesson, nor was He being vindictive. Your Father sees and understands your pain. He wants to comfort you and to heal you. Listen closely, because I believe He is saying, "I love you. It's going to be okay. I promise you will see My goodness again in this lifetime. You are going to be okay."

Tell Him how you feel. Ask Him to hold you close. Ask Him your hard questions. He has the ability to listen and even to answer. Trust Him.

SEEK THE GOODNESS OF THE LORD

I recommend keeping a list of even the smallest moments of progress you make in your journey, because they demonstrate the goodness of God. If you wake up breathing, write it down. If you are visited by a concerned friend, write it down. If you notice beauty in God's creation when you are outdoors, write it down. If you find humor in conversation . . . You get the idea. Over time, these little blessings will become a list of souvenirs of how God is working in your life—and those reminders are powerful!

Throughout the book of Psalms, David would pause to point out ways God has demonstrated His power (63:2), love (52:8–9), blessings (3:8), interventions (18:16–19), forgiveness (103:1–3), and other characteristics throughout David's own life. David also recalled the miracles God had performed throughout Scripture, and he revered God as the Creator of the heavens and the earth (8:3–8). David would list these things to remind himself not only that God can do more than we could ask or imagine but that God wants good for us.

CONTINUE TO LIVE LIFE

My brother's story has been such an inspiration to so many people. He began by speaking his confidence in the goodness of God, but then he continued to live as if he truly believed his words. During the years that his health declined, my brother told me he felt God was telling him to return to college to study for ministry. He didn't know what kind of ministry, but he knew he would need to have a deep understanding of Scripture and theology. Andy told me that if he had a successful transplant, he planned to enroll in Bible college as soon as he recovered.

It struck me that Andy felt called to ministry but only planned to begin his studies if and when he was healed. I asked, "Do you think God would call you to ministry if you were not going to be around to do ministry?" It was a rhetorical question. But my brother became very quiet.

About a week later, he called me. He said, "You're right."

"I am? What am I right about?" I didn't remember having any difference to settle.

Andy said, "God is clearly calling me to prepare for something. I can't work, but I can read and write. I am starting Bible college next month. I am going to get ready for whatever God has planned next and trust that He will use it as He sees fit."

My brother chose to place his trust in God and to faithfully live a life of purpose for as long as he was breathing. He did begin his studies right away. His health declined enough that he had to stop taking classes, but he didn't give up. He continued to study Scripture and to pray over his future ministry.

Though the rest of us were about to abandon hope that Andy would survive long enough for a lung transplant, he kept praying about his future. Then, in 2005, Andy underwent a successful double lung transplant. He continued his studies and has served as a leader in his church for several years. Although he returned to his work as a mechanical engineer, he regularly mentors and encourages others who are waiting for transplant surgeries. God indeed had a ministry plan for my brother, just as he had hoped.

Hope is the thing that keeps us moving forward. I leave you with these statements to ponder, because the words are sure and true:

God will not bring back all we have lost, but He will restore our joy.

God will not make us forget our traumatic events, but He will give us a deeper understanding.

God will not make us get over our trauma, but He will get us through it.

God exists, and He is good.

There is life after trauma. Live like this is true—because it is.

Questions for Reflection

1. What are some hard questions you have been afraid to confront God with?

2. What do you think the "goodness of the Lord" is? What do these words mean to you?

3. Begin a list of ways you have experienced the goodness of God in your lifetime.

*May the God of **hope** fill you with all joy and peace as you **trust** in him, so that you may overflow with **hope** by the power of the Holy Spirit.*

ROMANS 15:13

CHAPTER 11

Harnessing the Power of Persistence

*J*ohn 15 addresses the importance of branches staying connected to the vine. That sounds like the opposite of pruning, doesn't it? Two truths apply to vines—and to my pear tree. The first is that pruning helps the vine or tree grow stronger and produce more fruit. The second truth is that branches severed from the tree will never produce fruit. Pruning is good for the growth and health of the tree, but it is death to the branches that are removed.

Where am I going with this? Both truths apply to us too. (In using the metaphor of pruning, usually we're the tree; here, however, for the second truth, we'll view ourselves as a branch.) Let's consider Jesus's words in John 15:4: "Remain in me, as I also remain in you. No branch can bear fruit by itself; it must remain in the vine. Neither can you bear fruit unless you remain in me."

Jesus continues, "I am the vine; you are the branches" (verse 5). If that sounds confusing, let me break it down a bit. Jesus was saying that we need to stay connected to Him in order to bear fruit. And what does it mean to "bear fruit"? It means to produce sweet deliciousness that nourishes others. The book of Galatians tells us that the fruit of the Spirit is love, joy, peace, patience, kindness, goodness, faithfulness, gentleness, and self-control (5:22–23 ESV). Wow. That is a group of character traits I would love to possess, wouldn't you? What sweetness is produced when these character traits are on display.

When we are dealing with trauma, many of these characteristics seem far out of reach. Joy? Peace? Yes, please. Where can I get some of that patience and self-control? Love, kindness, goodness, and gentleness all would be a balm to my parched soul when I am at my lowest. I want to produce this fruit, don't you?

Some translations of the Bible, like the ESV, say the branches need to *abide* in the vine. I always thought the word *abide* meant to sit and rest. To abide in the Lord sounds to me like curling up in His presence and letting Him comfort me. I was surprised when I learned that the word *abide* is sometimes used as a synonym for the word *persist*. That word seems like the opposite of resting to me.

When our pear tree was injured, Barry and I could have simply dug it up and planted a new tree in its place, but we didn't. We decided to wait it out, and the tree persisted. The recovery would take time, but we were persistent during that time. We made sure the tree had consistent sunshine, space to grow, and plenty of water. This required a bit of work on our part, but we were consistent and faithful in doing what was necessary to heal the tree.

Healing requires persistence, and persistence takes work. This nugget of wisdom is key to healing the human spirit as well. Where the tree needed sunshine, we need hope; where the tree needed space, we need grace; and where the tree needed water, we need the Word of God.

In her memoir, *A Search for Purple Cows*, my dear friend Susan Call documents her story of surviving domestic violence.[1] Susan married a man who seemed confident and intelligent. As the marriage progressed, the couple had two children and stable jobs. Susan wanted to believe life was good.

Unfortunately, the same qualities that attracted Susan to her husband began to morph. His confidence and intelligence became weapons he wielded against his wife. He frequently told Susan she was stupid and worthless. He told her she was nothing without him, and it was only because of him that she had any value at all.

Healing requires persistence, and persistence takes work.

The circumstances worsened to the point that Susan felt she needed to leave the marriage for the safety of herself and her children, but her husband threatened to have her killed if she left. What followed was terrifying. Susan learned her husband indeed had some very dangerous contacts. When he placed a contract on her life, her story became surreal. Susan and her children had to plan an escape with the help of private investigators and law enforcement.

I asked Susan what it took for her to survive this ordeal and eventually find healing after the trauma. Her answer pointed toward persistence and consistent perseverance. Susan said, "Looking back, I realize that resilience was a by-product of the many small decisions I made daily: to keep going and to refuse to give up. It's far too easy to hold on to hurtful words that shake our sense of self-worth. When those words come from a spouse or someone we care about, they can be harder to shake. But with each answered prayer, the countless ways He provided for me and my children, and with the unexplainable peace He gave me in the middle of my storm, God showed me that He cares about me. He's always close. As I focused on Him, He helped me see my worth with new eyes."

I mentioned that my tree needed sunshine (hope), space (grace), and water (the Word). Let's take a closer look at how these concepts can help you abide and persist after trauma.

Hope

Susan said, "Without hope I never would have escaped my situation. I had to believe that the future could be better, or I would have given up." The hope of a safe future for her and her children gave her the courage to escape danger. She held on to the hope that things could be better outside of her relationship. She was persistent in reminding herself that she was valued by God and that God wouldn't want her to be unsafe. She knew that if she lost hope, she would quit trying to improve her circumstances.

Even after Susan and her kids escaped to safety, hope allowed her to live life forward rather than dwell in the past. Rather than looking at all that she had lost, including her home and financial security, she had great hope for her children and for her future. She settled into a small apartment and made it a comfortable, positive, safe home for her kids. She began to put small amounts of money away for her children's future education, even though her children were very young. Susan said she had to acknowledge the past, live in the present, and plan for the future. That is what hope does.

Grace

Susan had been told for years that she was worthless. It would have been easy to believe these lies after her escape. She had given up her home, financial security, and a network of friends who believed her husband was in fact the upstanding man his confidence portrayed. She could have wallowed in her losses and believed she had failed.

But instead of falling into the miry pit of shame and self-condemnation, Susan said she tried to see herself through a lens of grace each day. She reminded herself that she was a branch connected to a life-giving, fruit-producing Vine. To give herself space to heal, Susan knew she would have to be kind to herself, so every day she journaled. She wrote about the things she had accomplished that day, what she looked forward to accomplishing the next day, and how God had been nourishing her. Keeping track of the different ways the Vine had cared for the branch helped her to remember the faithfulness, power, and constant love of God.

While it is important to hope for the future, we still need to remember to walk through our grief, as mentioned in chapter 10. Susan had to give herself space to grieve. She often journaled about her grief and allowed herself to acknowledge her pain.

Susan also met weekly with a therapist to process all that had occurred. She found that she needed to forgive herself, because she felt she had made a terrible mistake in marrying her abuser. She persisted in meeting with her therapist as she processed her grief, forgave herself, and even learned to forgive her husband. This doesn't mean she reconciled with him; she simply arrived at a place where she could remember him without being consumed by anger.

I hope you are allowing yourself the space and grace to grieve your own trauma. Giving yourself grace includes being kind to yourself. Let go of the negative, stinkin' thinkin' that so often follows traumatic events. Do you find yourself beating yourself up over your past decisions? Devaluing yourself? This negative self-talk will never bring about healing. You have a God who created you with purpose and intention, and He loves you. It is time to persistently listen for His voice.

The Word

Susan also persistently read the Bible during her healing. As a branch, she stayed connected to the Vine. She didn't complete any major Bible studies or begin a preplanned daily reading schedule. During trauma, we don't often have the mental bandwidth to take on such long-term studies. Instead she kept it simple. She described opening her Bible and reading just a few verses each day, focusing on what God might have to say to her that day.

The first few days, Susan noticed her Bible fell open to the same verse each day. She took note and decided to memorize the verse. She found strength in these few words from God and would repeat the same verse each day as well as any time she was feeling weak. She began to crave reading her Bible and found that, like water, the words often quenched her spiritual thirst.

Susan wanted to abide in Jesus, to be connected to the strong Vine that provided for her every need. Often she would look to the book of Psalms for encouraging words or turn to Proverbs for advice on how to move forward. Abiding in the Word of God offered Susan the comfort, guidance, and reassurance she craved.

SCALING THE MOUNTAIN

Susan's story is a story of persistence. Following trauma, survival and healing can feel like an unscalable mountain. Anyone who has climbed a mountain will tell you it is done one step at a time, and that is also how we get through the aftermath of trauma.

Does your pain seem too heavy to bear right now? Is the situation you are facing overwhelming? Does it feel like the entire world is on your shoulders? If so, persistence may sound impossible. I want to encourage you to keep putting one foot in front of the other. You do not need to conquer the entire mountain today. If today you move forward only one inch, you have moved *forward*. If today feels like you have made no progress, but you have stood in place, then you have not moved *backward*.

> *You do not need to conquer the entire mountain today.*

The truth is, there will be days when you do feel you have taken a step backward. It's okay. This is when you give yourself grace. The journey to healing is not a steady climb. Some days will be harder than others. This may be a sign that it is time to refuel your body by resting and your soul by feeding on the Word of God.

It also may be a sign that you need a belayer—a climbing partner who controls the end of the safety rope as you climb the mountain. Have you identified people you trust to watch out for you as you make the climb? That support network is so important on the healing journey. On those days when you feel you are back-sliding, reach out to one of your belayers and let them know you are struggling to persist. There is no shame in having a belayer when climbing a mountain. These partners are essential to our success.

HOW TO PERSIST

Persistence means to keep trying even when something is difficult or when obstacles stand in the way. Trauma is difficult, and the obstacles may seem too numerous to conquer. So how do we persist?

- *Break your goal into small chunks.* A mountain climber will look at the summit from time to time while climbing. The summit represents the end goal; it inspires the climber to persist. But the main focus of the climber will always be on the current leg of the journey. To focus on the summit would be overwhelming and discouraging. The journey would look too far and difficult to manage, but one leg of the journey *is* manageable. The climber only needs to conquer one section each day, and eventually that person will reach the summit.

  That is how you need to view healing. Keep a hopeful eye on the summit but put your effort into only one step at a time. Each step moves you in the right direction. Compartmentalize as needed in order to stay focused (see chapter 7).

- *Obtain the right equipment.* Besides a belayer, a climber may need special shoes and spikes. He or she may require a warm blanket, a strong rope, a lightweight backpack, and other essentials. As you traverse the healing process, you too will need certain equipment. You will need a person or group of people you trust to support you. You may require community resources such as the police, the courts, medical professionals, a counselor, or clergy. You will need hope and grace. And don't forget to pack a Bible; it will be your road map.

- **Be strategic.** A climber needs to learn techniques and strategies for success before taking on a mountain. In chapters 8 and 9, we discussed some therapeutic and personal strategies that can help you make the climb. Intentionally put those strategies to work.

- **Trust.** You can get to the top of this mountain. You will not always be in the valley. God is bigger than any mountain you may face, and He wants to see you succeed.

- **Remain connected to the Vine.** Jesus said we need to abide (persist) in Him in order to bear fruit. The goal in the healing process is to cultivate the fruit of the Spirit—love, joy, peace, patience, kindness, goodness, faithfulness, gentleness, and self-control. Persistently seek the healing power of Jesus. He wants to produce this fruit in you. Remember that we need access to those deep roots in order to produce fruit.

I know there are times when it might seem easier to surrender. Trauma is ugly and painful. Please remember that the only way out is through. Persist in taking care of your basic needs. Persist in imagining a future that includes joy. Persist in trusting that you are not alone. Persist in remaining connected to the Vine. One step at a time and you will scale that "unscalable" mountain.

Questions for Reflection

1. What do you feel is your greatest obstacle to healing?

2. In what areas do you need to give yourself grace?

Let us hold tightly without wavering to the hope we affirm,
for God can be trusted to keep his promise.

HEBREWS 10:23 (NLT)

PART III

Avoiding Retraumatization

CHAPTER 12

When People Say the Wrong Thing

When you are suffering, people may not know what to say. Insensitive and poorly framed comments can cause you to feel set back. Don't be discouraged—this is normal. And you can rise above hurtful comments like these with a few strategies.

My husband's and my pear tree was injured when my husband tried to remove a larger tree that was casting shade on it. Our goal was to give the little pear the room and sunshine it needed to flourish and bloom. My husband had good intentions when he cut down the big pine, but he inadvertently harmed the pear tree when he miscalculated the angle of the pine tree.

MISCALCULATED COMMENTS

Have you ever meant well but miscalculated the result of your words? I have! When I was a teen, I attended the funeral of a young woman named Midge. She had been one of my babysitters when I was a child, and her mother was my mother's close friend. Midge was beautiful, kind, and vibrant. When she died of cancer, it was my first experience with grief and loss. Standing in line at her funeral, I knew

I would need to say something to Midge's mother. I had heard there were right and wrong things to say at a funeral, but I had no idea what a right thing would be. Pondering what to say, I became more and more nervous. When my turn came, I hugged Midge's mom and said, "You were so lucky to be her mom and to know her so well."

Midge's mom looked horrified. She began to cry even harder. "Lucky?" she said. "I wish I had never known her at all. This would be much easier if she had been a stranger." Her pain was palpable.

I felt embarrassed and ashamed for my insensitive comment. Why couldn't I have simply stuck with "I'm sorry for your loss"? This was when I learned that meaning well doesn't always give us the right words. I also learned that sometimes there are no right words. In the face of grief and pain, words simply fall short. Thankfully, Midge's mom forgave my naivete.

Often when people say the wrong thing, it is a simple miscalculation. In the awkwardness, pain, and confusion of the moment, people search for the right thing to say, but the right thing is elusive. In the aftermath of trauma, we are without a compass or a map. And those around us are too. They have no idea how to navigate our pain . . . or their own.

Remember when we talked about the stages of grief and how they apply to trauma recovery? As we bounce around between denial, shock, sadness, and anger, we naturally become inwardly focused on our own pain and survival. This sets us up for the perfect storm. We forget that those around us are experiencing their own confusion and pain. So when they say something that stomps on our pain, we tend to quickly jump into the anger part of the grief cycle. This is an unfortunate but normal part of surviving.

My words to Midge's mom stomped on her shock and denial. She was not prepared to think about the happy memories of Midge yet; she was still trying to make sense of her loss. My unwise comment was likely retraumatizing to this poor woman. Although I was young and meant well, she responded in anger. In that moment, it was a natural response, and it was okay. Some might think it was rude for her to be angry at a young person who meant well, but this was not rudeness. It was survival.

THE RING THEORY

One theory offers guidelines for communicating with those impacted by trauma. The ring theory was originally presented by Susan Silk and Barry Goldman.[1] Think of those who have been impacted by trauma as existing in concentric rings, like a target. The person or people who have directly experienced the trauma are in the center ring—the bull's-eye. They deserve and need grace, space, and an embrace. Midge's mother, father, husband, and children stood in the bull's-eye.

> *The person or people who have directly experienced the trauma deserve and need grace, space, and an embrace.*

The person or people in that inner ring, closest to the pain, get to say and feel anything they need to say and feel, whenever they want, and to whoever stands outside the bull's-eye. It is the only advantage of being in the bull's-eye. That person in the bull's-eye can't be expected to comfort those in the outer circles. They are allowed to *dump out*. They can complain, scream that life isn't fair, spew anger, and curse the heavens out loud.

Everyone else has the right to dump too, but only to those who stand in larger rings. When we are talking to someone who stands closer to the center of the crisis, our goal should be to comfort, listen, and help. We may be thinking of all the sadness, pain, and anger we feel, but we should never expect a person in a smaller ring to comfort us. The idea is that we *comfort in* and *dump out*.

My Interpretation of Silk and Goldman's Ring Theory

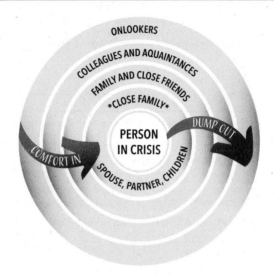

In the example of Midge's funeral, I would have likely fallen into the ring of acquaintances. Midge's mom was the person in crisis. When my words touched a nerve, she dumped out. I was attempting to comfort in, but she interpreted the words differently—and it was okay that she did so.

If you are standing in the bull's-eye and respond strongly to well-meant words, give yourself grace. Focus on surviving. If later you regret your response, you can always apologize. Forgiveness is freeing for all parties involved. Midge's mom apologized, and I did the same. We forgave each other, and God knew our hearts.

INSENSITIVE WORDS

In the previous example, the words were meant to comfort but were miscalculated. But sometimes people say things that are out of order, dumping on people in inner circles. I met a couple who learned midway through a pregnancy that their child would not survive outside the womb. This news placed the expectant parents squarely in the bull's-eye. As the community learned of the tragedy, one pregnant woman dumped in without realizing it.

This young woman naturally became concerned for her own unborn child. She poured her worry out on the already-traumatized woman. "That terrifies me! I don't think I could handle it if I learned my baby wasn't going to live."

She was sharing her deepest thoughts with the wrong person. Her fear was valid, and she had every right to dump out by speaking to her spouse and friends who stood in larger circles, but she inadvertently dumped her momentary stress into someone else's big "T" Trauma bull's-eye, lacking sensitivity.

The pregnant woman had made the loss about herself. I don't know how the woman I know responded in the moment, but I remember her later sharing her hurt. She said, "I tried to listen to her, but I couldn't believe she made it about her. I don't think I can handle this either. I can't possibly think about her fears when my own are staring me in the eye."

When you are standing in the bull's-eye and others speak out of order, again, give yourself grace. It is not your responsibility to comfort others. If you can, let those comments go. Those people will find others to comfort them. If you respond strongly, it's okay. You are in the bull's-eye. It is not your turn to be the comforter. Not now. A time will come when you stand in a larger circle and have opportunity to comfort others, but this isn't it.

WHEN PEOPLE GIVE ADVICE

Why, oh why, do we human beings feel the need to fix things? As a trauma survivor, you have likely had many people offer you well-meaning advice. When the unthinkable happens, human nature makes us want to find answers and solutions. Sometimes we want solutions to stop the pain, but often we simply want answers to make sense of the chaos and carnage.

The story of Job is one of big "T" Trauma that happened in the life of a good man. Job lost his home, his children, his reputation, health, wealth, and more. As he stood in the bull's-eye, three friends—Eliphaz, Bildad, and Zophar—came to comfort him. For seven days they sat on the ground in silence with Job, crying with their friend and allowing him to experience the full measure of his grief. For seven days they did exactly the right thing.

I imagine that as they sat in silence, Job's friends did a lot of thinking. Their friend's trauma was enormous. They must have thought, *Why Job?* I am sure they wished he had been spared. Job's devastation might have led them to think, *What if it were me?* That in turn would likely have led them to wonder, Why *had* these things happened to Job? What were the reasons these things could not happen to them too? Job's friends were trying to make sense of the chaos so they could avoid a similar experience, and they had seven days of silence to overthink the matter.

The Bible tells us Job was a good man, but his friends began to wonder if God was punishing Job for something. So after seven days of wisely remaining silent, Job's friends began to say the wrong things. Each of the three spoke at length about why Job was suffering. Unfortunately, the friends reasoned that Job had done something wrong. They held an inaccurate view of the character of God, seeing Him as an angry, severe disciplinarian, and failed to acknowledge that God is love.

Although Job insisted he was innocent, his friends battered him with unsolicited advice. They repeatedly counseled Job to admit his wrongdoing and change his ways so God would cease the punishment.

I love the way in which God finally clarified who He is and how He works. God spoke to Job and his friends "out of the whirlwind" (Job 38:1; 40:6 KJV). And what did God say? In short, "Who are you to talk?" He then went on to tell Job not to take the advice of his friends. Can you imagine? The friends were put in their place by the God of the universe! They must have been humiliated and terrified.

There is an interesting twist in Job's story. His friends returned to him and asked him to pray for them. Even after the way they had retraumatized him, Job chose to forgive them. He prayed for his friends and asked God to forgive and bless them. Job prayed, and God restored Job's wealth and livelihood. In fact, God gave him twice as much as he had before. Job's reputation was restored. He went on to live one hundred forty more years. And while his children could not be restored, he found joy in ten more children and many grandchildren. Job clearly had much grief to walk through, but he did see the goodness of the Lord in the land of the living.

I hope you will consider reading the book of Job at some point in your healing process—maybe later in your journey. We can learn so much about the nature of God and His healing goodness from this story. One day you may find purpose in the journey. Hold on to the hope that is found in God's power and love.

CLICHÉ COMFORT

"You'll get over this."

"This too shall pass."

"It could have been worse."

"Look on the bright side."

"Others have it worse than you do."

Clichés like these are meant to comfort, but they don't. They aim to show you that there is a continuum of pain, and you are better off than you think. But they just end up minimizing your hurt.

When your present pain is worse than anything you ever have or likely ever will experience, hypothetical bright sides or comparisons to other people's hurts will not make you feel better. People who say such things fail to recognize the depth of your suffering. I am so sorry. Once again, I suggest that you imagine yourself standing in the bull's-eye. Allow yourself to experience regret, fear, grief, pain, and everything you are feeling. Your story is *your* story. No one else's story is better or worse than yours; no other worst-case scenario will make your experience seem better. Please don't attempt to comfort yourself with it-could-be-worse statements. Give your story the respect it deserves. Give your emotions space.

> *Please don't attempt to comfort yourself with it-could-be-worse statements. Give your story the respect it deserves.*

Other unhelpful clichés stem from people trying to relate to you. "I have a friend who went through the same thing, and she got over it." The problem is, a statement like this makes a faulty comparison. No two people experience trauma the same way. Our reactions to trauma vary based on our taproots and root systems, our personalities, our support systems, and our coping skills.[2]

You may also hear statements such as "When will you get over this?" and "It's been years since this happened to you." But again, we don't get *over* trauma, and getting *through* it has no set timeline. If someone frequently says such things, you may need to prune that relationship for a while. He or she likely has a small tolerance for your pain and is not a strong support for you. While you are in the struggle, it is important that you surround yourself with people who will love on you and encourage you. This isn't to say you should end a friendship with a person who makes such statements; the person simply may not have the skills to be a part of your support system at this time.

Remember that unprocessed trauma can live in your amygdala for a lifetime.

Healing is possible, but how long it takes can vary greatly. In the meantime, commit to doing the things that will lead to healing, but don't let others rush you. One step at a time.

My husband frequently (and jokingly) asks me how to eat an elephant. The answer is, One bite at a time. We have talked about compartmentalizing and scaling the mountain one step at a time; the elephant is another metaphor for that same idea. Remember, there is no timeline for healing. One man who suffered trauma said he would give the healing process three months. He deemed this an acceptable amount of time to grieve and that there was no excuse for dwelling on the incident after that. I probably don't have to tell you that he was disappointed in himself after the three months had passed.

How long will it take to heal? As long as it takes. I know I could eat an elephant more easily if I were given a year to do it rather than a day. Give yourself grace—but keep eating. It might seem like the journey will never end, but one day you will find that you have made more progress than you thought possible.

A CAVEAT TO CONSIDER

When people say the wrong things—and they will—remember this: Whether they miscalculated how their comments would land, or they dumped in, or said something insensitive, or used a minimizing cliché, or implied that you should "get over it," they probably are not aware how their words have stung your heart. While you might feel angry or hurt or defensive, the speaker may have no idea they said the wrong thing.

Good relationships have ended following trauma because of this dynamic. Marriages have fractured when spouses grieved differently and said the wrong things to each other. Friendships have died over misunderstandings and a perceived lack of support. People have distanced themselves from others whose good intentions fell short. Often this leads to further trauma, or retraumatization, for those involved.

GIVE YOURSELF TIME TO PROCESS

Initially, while you are standing in the bull's-eye, you will not have the same control over your responses as usual. Don't be hard on yourself in the moment. But as time goes on, you may find yourself looking back with regret over your reactions. That is okay too. Remember, you can always go back and apologize. Doing so may help you move forward in your healing and also may help those in the larger rings learn about the importance of words and how to comfort others.

If the person who spoke hurtful words does not accept the responsibility for those words, the process might include setting boundaries or pruning that relationship. Some people, when confronted with the pain their words caused, will blame you and say you're making it all about yourself.

Of *course* it is about you. You're standing in the bull's-eye. But narcissism may prevent them from ever understanding your point of view. Once you accept that reality, you can learn to set boundaries. You can respectfully refuse to accept responsibility for their actions.

When you are standing in the bull's-eye, you are more vulnerable to anger because anger is a part of the grieving process. You don't want to end good relationships in the heat of the moment over one insensitive comment. But while we do not want to lose good relationships over words, over time we may learn that a relationship is unhealthy. Unfortunately, if you find a relationship is toxic, it may become necessary to end or limit that relationship indefinitely.

Begin with setting boundaries. If boundaries are repeatedly breached or not respected, the relationship might be toxic. Toxic relationships are defined by ongoing patterns of unhealthy behavior. If you've tried to create healthy circumstances by setting boundaries but harmful patterns persist, you may need to prune. Ask yourself: Will it bring more trauma for *you* to continue the relationship or to end it?

Prioritize protecting yourself from further trauma. I have seen many people continue to be hurt in toxic relationships because they don't want to disappoint the other person. Don't let guilt hold you hostage. Guilt stands in the way of healthy boundary setting and necessary pruning. Stand firm. You can always reconsider your boundaries if you see growth in the other person.

> *If boundaries are repeatedly breached or not respected, the relationship might be toxic.*

I pray you will find healing in your relationships as you talk to your friends about how their words hurt you. I believe that in many cases, misunderstandings can be sorted out, lessons can be learned on both sides, and strong relationships can survive. Your close relationships are precious and deserve to be protected, but relationships that hinder your healing over time are another story. Protect your heart, friend.

Questions for Reflection

1. What things have people said to you that still cause unease? If possible, imagine what they might have intended with the words.

2. Is there a next step you might need or want to take in bringing understanding to the situation?

*Everyone enjoys a fitting reply; it is wonderful to say
the right thing at the right time!*

PROVERBS 15:23 (NLT)

CHAPTER 13

Guilt and Shame

Miscalculated and insensitive comments are common and painful. Comments meant to blame or shame are toxic in and of themselves. Trauma survivors commonly experience guilt or shame following the event. Human nature is to try to make sense of the unimaginable. We look back and ask ourselves what might have prevented the trauma. *What if I had noticed the red flags? What if I had intervened sooner? Could I have stopped this from happening? Why didn't I say xyz?* While such thoughts naturally arise during the coping process, they can lead to feelings of shame if unchecked. Regardless of whether shame comes from external sources or arises from within, it is not conducive to healing. Let's dive into this deeply.

THE DIFFERENCE BETWEEN GUILT AND SHAME

We often use the terms guilt and shame interchangeably, but the difference between the two is profound and important to recognize. Guilt stems from a specific action, for which we accept responsibility. Guilt says, "I have done something unacceptable." If we have hurt someone with our words or done something we believe was wrong, we are guilty. Shame, however, says, "I am unacceptable." While guilt focuses on behavior, shame focuses on self. Shame crushes the soul.

Brené Brown writes and lectures on vulnerability. In her book *I Thought It Was*

Just Me (but It Isn't), she writes, "Shame corrodes the very part of us that believes we are capable of change."[1] Think about that. When a person *makes* a mistake, they have ways to resolve the guilt. They can apologize, fix the damage that has been done, or make amends in some way. But when a person believes they *are* a mistake, what options do they have? Shame often leads to low self-esteem, depression, and hopelessness. Shame is far more debilitating than guilt.

SHAMING THE SELF

The shift from guilt to shame following trauma happens when we move from thoughts like *I wish I hadn't gotten drunk that night* to *I'm an idiot, so of course I got drunk that night*. When post-traumatic guilt morphs into self-shaming, it will interfere with the healing process. Blaming and shaming ourselves saps us of the energy we need to move forward. Shame chains us to our feelings of failure and prevents us from stepping into a hopeful future. Some people dwell in the valley of shame for a lifetime, feeling they do not deserve to be comforted, loved, or healed.

> *Guilt says, "I have done something unacceptable." Shame says, "I am unacceptable."*

Many of us have placed ourselves in that valley. While others tell us we are not to blame, tell us we didn't deserve our pain, and try to comfort us, we reject their words because we have already condemned ourselves. Drawn inward to shame by our own stinkin' thinkin', we are unable to accept the outward grace others offer, or to give ourselves grace.

A senior in high school, "Brad" was shy and insecure. Though he was a talented musician, he had no plan at all for his life beyond graduation. He shared that he saw no future for himself because he had nothing to offer the world. He had been thinking about suicide as an option.

His parents, however, stated that Brad had been threatening suicide for years. In their opinion he was seeking attention and would never follow through. Over the next several months, I talked with Brad's parents often, but they continued to insist that their son was not capable of taking his own life.

Three months after Brad graduated, he followed through. His parents' grief was compounded by immense feelings of shame. Of course they blamed themselves for ignoring the warning signs—following a suicide, it is common for families and friends to experience survivor's guilt. But this circumstance was particularly agonizing. These parents had been made aware of the potential and yet failed to intervene. Both said they could never forgive themselves. But letting go of shame was exactly what they needed to do to find peace.

Brad's parents made a mistake in not getting help for their son, but they were not evil people. As is common for parents, they couldn't believe that their child might actually take his own life. Their response was due to denial and avoidance of the inconceivable truth that their son was in danger. Denial and avoidance are part of the human condition. After Brad's death, his parents felt they didn't deserve to be released from their pain. Shame was the jail they locked themselves in as punishment for what they believed was their horrific crime.

What about you? Have you invited shame to live in your soul following trauma? Does a part of your trauma story include a decision you regret or a mistake you made? Have you imprisoned yourself because of your choices?

If so, please understand that God does not want this for you. When God created you, He did not make a mistake. In your humanness, you may make mistakes, but you yourself are not a mistake. Jesus took the punishment for our sins on the cross knowing full well that we would fall short at times. You are forgiven because of His love for you, and He will never stop loving you.

If the all-powerful, all-knowing God of the universe has forgiven you and set you free from all condemnation, why are you keeping yourself in a prison of self-deprecation and contempt? Your jail door is not locked. Set yourself free.

FREEING YOURSELF FROM SHAME

There are a few things you can do to free yourself from shame. First, challenge the logic of your thought patterns. For example, ask yourself what evidence proves your negative thoughts to be true. In the case of Brad's parents, there was no evidence they were responsible for his death. What *was* true was that the only person controlling Brad's behavior was Brad. Even if they had responded differently to the warning signs, Brad might still have made the same choices.

Another way you can let go of shame is to imagine what you would tell a friend in the same situation. When shame pulls all thoughts inward, this practice forces you to think outside yourself. Often we blame and shame ourselves in ways we would never do to others. If Brad's parents were talking to a friend who lost a child to suicide, would they tell that parent it was his or her own fault? I highly doubt it. They would want to comfort and support their grieving friend.

Shame's only mode of operating is negativity. The voice of shame tells us we are faulty, flawed, incompetent, and unworthy. It is a voice of judgment. To silence that voice, we must intentionally speak positive messages to ourselves. When the voice of the Enemy says, "This is your fault," you might respond with, "I had no power to prevent it." When the voice says, "You are worthless," respond with, "God says I am worthy."

It might be difficult to think of positive responses when you are feeling shame. If this is the case, consider asking a close friend, family member, or therapist to help you. Share with them how you are feeling and allow them to speak truth into your heart.

BLAME AND SHAME FROM OTHERS

Some of the clichés and comments discussed in the last chapter may cause us to shame ourselves, but sometimes others will overtly and maliciously blame us for our crisis. That seems incomprehensible, doesn't it? Yet it's quite common with certain traumas, especially sexual trauma. Blaming and shaming the victim may arise when someone who knows the perpetrator doesn't want to believe that person is capable of his or her behavior. Or, as in the case of Job's friends, the blamer could be reassuring himself, telling himself that if he can just figure out what the sufferer did wrong, he can modify his own behavior and ensure nothing similar will ever befall him. For the few survivors who face their perpetrator in court, the defense can be brutal. Typically, the defense will try to prove one of two things: that either the survivor is lying or the survivor caused the abuse to happen. The survivor endures being blamed, shamed, and called a liar.

I loathe having to say these things in this book. If you have experienced sexual trauma, I am so sorry for the pain my words may elicit. Sexual abuse and assault are the most underreported crimes in our nation for a reason: shame. I would love to see them reported and prosecuted more, but I understand the reluctance. The most important message I want you to hear is this:

IT WAS NOT YOUR FAULT.

How can I say that when I don't know your circumstances? What if you were drinking, or flirting, or dressed scantily, or promiscuous, or . . . ? Once again—and please hear this loud and clear:

If you were not an adult, or if you did not give consent, it was not your fault.

When I was attacked in college, the man was able to get into my room because the door was unlocked. An unusual set of circumstances that I won't get into led to that lapse in security. When I left for college, my mom had worried that I wouldn't lock my door at night, and I rolled my eyes at her. "Mom, I will be fine! Nothing is going to happen." But I also promised to keep my door locked. I failed to keep that promise, and I felt guilty.

Following the attack, I spent the entire Saturday in the hospital. Sunday, I moved out of my room and into another. Monday, I returned to class as if nothing had happened. I just wanted to return to normal. Unfortunately, my subconscious knew that things were not normal anymore. I was nervous and hypervigilant. As I walked to class, I scanned the crowds, wondering if my attacker might be walking the same sidewalk I was. My hypervigilance increased halfway through the week when the story of my attack appeared on the front page of the campus newspaper. The masked man had told me he would come after me if anything showed up in the paper.

I saw the article Wednesday morning as I was preparing to walk to class. The details were kept to a minimum, and I was not named. Praise God for that. Walking to class that morning took great focus and determination. As I walked into the building of my class, I heard people talking about the article. Because of the violent nature of the crime and because it took place on campus, the news stirred fear in the student body. It seemed like everyone was talking about it. And it felt like everyone was looking at me, but that was not the truth. No one knew I had been the victim.

I hurried to my class and took a seat, trying to ignore the chatter that seemed to echo all around me. Two students walked into the classroom and sat behind me. One said, "Did you hear about that girl who was attacked on campus?"

I wanted to put my hands over my ears and start singing loudly, but I didn't want to be conspicuous. I never got the chance. I heard the other student respond, "She was so stupid! It's her own fault for not locking the door."

My heart began to beat so fast and hard I was afraid the two students would hear it. The room seemed to spin before my eyes. I quickly packed my books into my bag and snuck out of the room. I walked home as quickly as I could, hoping no one would notice my tears, because I didn't want to explain myself. I didn't want anyone to know I was the stupid girl who had failed to lock my door.

I don't recall if I missed any other classes that week, but I certainly missed that one. My guilt for not locking the door had turned to shame. I was undone. *

As I struggled with the fear, pain, and grief of my situation, I was now experiencing shame as well. But the circumstances that led to my door being unlocked were human error. If you are human, you have made errors and mistakes too. My classmate was wrong to blame me for the decisions of the man who entered my room that night. He and he alone was responsible for his actions, regardless of any errors on my part. Something similar may also be true in your trauma story.

Following a trauma, the words of others can be retraumatizing and dangerous. How do you protect yourself? Are you struggling with someone who is blaming and shaming you for your trauma?

If so, I want you to remember the boundaries from Cloud and Townsend that we discussed in chapter 7, and to pause and walk through the following exercise.

Close your eyes and picture a neighborhood with clearly drawn property lines. Imagine which property is yours and which belongs to the person who has shamed you. Now ask yourself, Whose property does this problem live on?

Imagine what the blame and shame looks like. Is it a large pile of garbage? A huge tangle of weeds? However you choose to represent the blaming and shaming, picture it on the other person's property. Can you imagine a huge fence around that problem?

Once you have this image in your mind, I want you to leave the pile there and return to your own property. The wall leaves no way for this person's problem to spill into your space. Let it go.

When shame from others threatens to spill onto your property in the future, bring this image back to mind. You may have to do this frequently at first, but be persistent. Over time, your mind will begin to accept the truth that their shaming does not belong to you.

ACCEPTING THE WATER

Immediately after our pear tree was injured, we made sure to keep it watered well. It didn't need much attention before the trauma, but afterward, water was essential in supporting its new growth. The same can be said for us. We desperately need *living* water when we are injured, especially when we are experiencing shame.

Jesus described living water in the book of John, chapter 4. Jesus found a Samaritan woman drawing water from a well. This woman was living with shame—shame from her community and shame from within—but Jesus treated her with great respect. He asked her to draw some water for Him. This surprised the woman, first because she was a Samaritan and He was a Jew. Discrimination was alive and well when Jesus walked this planet; Jews didn't associate with Samaritans. In addition, the woman was bewildered because she had been married five times and was living with a man she wasn't married to, a situation Jews would not tolerate. Even her neighbors didn't associate with her. I imagine she didn't feel worthy of being acknowledged by this stranger.

The woman asked Jesus how he could even ask her for a drink. Jesus answered, "If you knew the generosity of God and who I am, you would be asking *me* for a drink, and I would give you fresh, living water" (John 4:10 MSG, emphasis in the original). Jesus was referring to Himself as living water! He told the woman that if she drank the living water, she would never be thirsty again.

Jesus knew everything about the Samaritan woman, yet He was unfazed by her shame. And as with her, Jesus offers us His love and grace regardless of our worthiness. He sees past our shame and guilt and offers to sustain us through difficult times.

There are many ways Jesus upholds us, but when we feel unworthy, we sometimes avoid the gifts He offers—especially reading the Bible and going to church. We don't want to be judged, and we don't want to be held accountable for what we believe is our failure.

> *Jesus offers us His love and grace regardless of our worthiness.*

But like my pear tree that needed water, we need living water to support new growth when we are wounded. Without water, we die.

AVOIDING THE WORD

Where can we find the living water Jesus spoke of? In the Word of God. Following trauma, it might seem like too big a task to read your Bible. That's okay. There are many things you can do to connect with God in small but powerful ways.

Try reading a daily devotional. If you don't already have one, just enter "devotional for trauma" in any web browser. You will find dozens of options. You can also purchase devotionals anywhere Christian books are sold. And you can likely find free devotionals through your local church.

Each short daily reading will guide you through a message of spiritual growth. Think of it as having coffee with God—it doesn't take long, but it's a great way to connect. The truths and stories contained in devotionals will open your eyes to small ways God's Word pertains to your day. Try to set aside fifteen minutes each day to read, pray, and sit in silence with God. As you meditate, ask God to reveal how He thinks about you. Your true identity is not trauma or shame. You are precious in God's eyes. You are his child, and He loves you completely.

R.A.W. journaling is another bite-size way to incorporate Scripture into your day. We discussed this approach in chapter 9 (see pages 100–101). The final step in the R.A.W. process is to search for a Scripture verse or two about each theme you journaled about. As you write the verses in your journal, you are inviting living water onto the pages.

Some avoid Scripture because they fear judgment. If fear of judgment is holding you back, you might want to begin by reading the book of Psalms.

A small group or personal Bible study can guide you in diving more deeply into Scripture. Group studies encourage questions and discussion that can lead to amazing insight and new perspective.

Others avoid Scripture simply because they don't know where to begin. But don't let the idea of reading the Bible overwhelm you. These ideas will help you digest Scripture one small bite at a time—like eating an elephant (remember?). I have a Bible verse of the day sent to my phone. Each morning, I read the verse before my feet hit the floor. There are several apps that send verse of the day content, and some provide mini lessons to go with each verse. The apps I recommend are the Bible App, YouVersion, and Bible Gateway. Each of these is free and safe to use.

AVOIDING CHURCH

People avoid church for many reasons following trauma. Is that you? Maybe you don't want to face people's questions, or you carry a bag so full of shame you don't think it will fit through the front door. Perhaps you just thirst for privacy and peace. But as counterintuitive as it may seem, surrounding yourself with people who represent the love of Jesus is one way to quench that thirst. Walking into a room full of people who may be concerned for you or who you feel might judge you takes courage and trust, because it puts you in a vulnerable place.

Remember, though, that Jesus sees your vulnerability, just like he saw the Samaritan woman's. Jesus is not blaming and shaming you, and neither should His people. Ignore the negative voice that says you are undeserving of compassion and empathy. The voice of God is whispering that you are precious. He wants to use His people to comfort and encourage you. In this way, the Father can hold you in His arms, gently loving you and soothing your wounds.

WHEN CHURCH IS THE PROBLEM

If your church is a place that causes you pain, this pain is not from God. Remember, our churches are full of broken people. Even our pastors are mere humans, flawed and imperfect. I don't say this to excuse church-inflicted hurt. I'm just saying it is not a reflection of God; it is a reflection of humanity. The church is supposed to be the hands and feet of Jesus when we are in pain. If your church is not living up to that, please don't blame God.

Perhaps your trauma occurred in the context of church, or maybe you have felt hurt by your church's response, or lack of response, to your pain. Either way, wounding in church can result in people's rejecting church, or even God, altogether. How can you find living water when your church seems like a desert wasteland?

Don't isolate yourself from other believers. If you choose to continue attending your church, hold your boundaries firm. Remember you are in the bull's-eye, and it is okay to expect people to try to comfort you during your season of healing. There is no shame in this.

While I don't recommend that people jump from church to church whenever things get tough, if you have experienced church hurt, it might be time to visit other churches. If you opt to do this, you do not need to let that decision add to your guilt and shame. When you find a good fit, worshiping with others can be a healing balm. Search for a church where you feel welcomed and accepted.

It's tempting to avoid God because of shame, but I encourage you to be persistent to remain in him. Whether you are looking for small ways to connect with God or for a safe group of people to worship with, try several options until you find one that works for you. Find your fit, but fit God in. He is the living water that can wash over you with waves of healing love. The antidote to shame is experiencing the unconditional, forgiving, empathetic, all-consuming, radically accepting love of God.

Questions for Reflection

1. Has shame taken up residence in your soul? If so, what has caused you to feel ashamed?

2. Who does God say you are?

3. What is one way you are, or will be, including Scripture reading into your day?

Now there is no condemnation for those who belong to Christ Jesus.

ROMANS 8:1 (NLT)

PART IV

Life Beyond Trauma

CHAPTER 14

Post-Traumatic Growth

In chapter 9, I talked about my deep desire for justice and closure when my cold case was reopened. At that time, I couldn't fathom why God would allow my wounds to be torn open again after so many years of successfully stuffing my pain away. As I searched for purpose, the only acceptable answer I could come up with was that my attacker was finally going to be arrested and put behind bars. He would be found guilty, and I would be the victor. I would get closure.

But that is not how things turned out. God is just, and I trust justice will be served in His way and timing, but I don't believe we're promised closure following trauma in this lifetime. Even if my perpetrator had been arrested, convicted, and sent to prison, would I really have experienced closure? I might have been grateful for justice, but it wouldn't have changed the fact that trauma had occurred. That experience will always be a part of my story, and it has impacted me in ways that will not be undone in this lifetime.

Everything we experience in life becomes a part of who we are. I believe God is offering us something even better than closure. He is offering growth.

Let me tell you the rest of the story of our little pear tree. It did far more than survive its first winter. It grew to become the fullest, most beautiful tree on our street. I am not exaggerating! By the second winter, I could no longer cover its branches with a garbage bag. In fact, I couldn't have reached its top with the longest ladder available. New branches formed to create the most perfectly shaped flowering tree I have ever seen. Not only was our New Bradford Pear the first to flower in the springtime, but it was absolutely engulfed in fluffy white flowers that caught the sun and reflected it back to the sky a hundredfold. Neighbors commented on its beauty and fragrance.

> *God is offering us something even better than closure. He is offering growth.*

The same year we planted the pear tree, our community planted flowering trees throughout our neighborhood. All of them were lovely, but our pear tree most definitely became the star of the show.

When fall arrived, the pear tree showed off with bright red and yellow leaves that resembled a blaze of warmth. It was magnificent! Its colors were the first to appear in early autumn, and its leaves were the last to fall. Our pear was quite a spectacle throughout the seasons.

We later learned that the tree had flourished *because* of the adversity it had faced. Its limbs strengthened, and it became more efficient at utilizing the nourishment from the sun and water because it had to work harder after the trauma. The tree didn't simply survive. It grew stronger and more beautiful than it would have without the trauma.

Guess what? Post-traumatic growth (PTG) is for real! Researchers have found that half to two-thirds of those who experience trauma grow through the experience.[1] Everyone has the potential for PTG. Research shows that growth is dependent on several things: coping skills, an understanding of trauma, the ability to accept support from others, strong taproots, a deep root system, and faith in a loving God. I pray you will grow in such a way that you not only will let yourself experience the goodness of the Lord in this lifetime but will have a deeper, richer appreciation for that goodness. Let's turn to an example in the first book of the Bible, Genesis, to see how this happened for a biblical figure.

THE EXAMPLE OF JOSEPH

The story I want to highlight is of Joseph and his post-traumatic growth. This Joseph is not the man who married Mary, the mother of Jesus. This Joseph lived long before Jesus was born. He had a boatload of brothers, and their father was Jacob.

As a young boy, Joseph seemed to have things pretty good. He was the favorite son. Most of us have heard about Joseph and his coat of many colors. Joseph's dad gave him that coat, and his brothers were jealous. Envy had been building in them a long time because of their father's favoritism. And then came the dreams. Despite being the next-to-youngest of the brothers, Joseph dreamed that his older brothers would one day bow down to him.

Joseph's older brothers despised him. They teased and mocked him initially, but the abuse eventually became physical. When Joseph told the brothers of his dreams that he would rule over them one day, they decided to kill him. When Joseph was seventeen, his brothers stole his fancy coat and threw him into a deep cistern with the intention of killing him. The oldest brother, Reuben, talked the others out of killing Joseph. Instead, they sold Joseph into slavery and convinced their father that Joseph had been killed by a wild animal.

If that wasn't trauma enough for Joseph, he was then sexually harassed by his master's wife, falsely accused of assault, and thrown into prison, where he remained until he was thirty years old. Joseph was a man of integrity. He had worked hard and always kept his master's best interest in mind. But the lies of the master's wife ruined his good reputation.

While in prison, Joseph remained trustworthy and reliable. The Bible says God was with Joseph the whole time. He continued to have dreams while he was in prison, and he learned that God had given him a gift: Joseph was able to interpret his dreams precisely. The story is long and interesting, but in short, the same dreaming that got Joseph in trouble with his brothers eventually led him to a position of second-in-command to the pharaoh of Egypt.

When the entire region languished under a severe famine as Joseph had predicted, his brothers and father faced starvation. Having no idea what had become of Joseph, his older brothers traveled to Egypt to buy grain for their family. Guess whom they had to bow before in their begging!

Joseph could easily have taken revenge on his brothers for the trauma they inflicted on him. He could have refused them food. He could have had them killed on the spot. Instead, Joseph forgave them, sent for his father, and provided his family with everything they needed. He went beyond forgiveness and reconciled with his brothers. They and their father were invited to move to Egypt, where Joseph gave all of them land for themselves and their livestock. Joseph chose to bless his family.[2]

Scripture says that what the brothers had intended for evil, God intended for good (Genesis 50:20). It doesn't say God caused Joseph's trauma, nor does it say the trauma was the reason Joseph experienced the goodness of the Lord. Joseph's story demonstrates that although God doesn't purpose for us to experience trauma, He can use anything for his purposes if we let Him. I *love* that. God was faithful to Joseph, and Joseph was faithful to God. As a result, God was able to use Joseph in powerful ways.

Joseph suffered for decades because of his brothers' actions, yet he extended love to them. His story offers us a beautiful example of post-traumatic growth. Had Joseph not grown through the horrible trauma of his earlier years, his story could have gone much differently. He might have become a resentful, bitter prisoner.

He might have been so angry at God that he refused to use his gift of interpreting dreams. He might have given in to the wife of his master and been killed for doing so. He might have given up while he was in prison. Yet Joseph rose above it all.

> *Scripture doesn't say God caused Joseph's trauma, nor does it say the trauma was the reason Joseph experienced the goodness of the Lord.*

Joseph's growth after trauma was clear and measurable. I am excited to tell you that your growth can be measured too!

MEASURING GROWTH

The post-traumatic growth inventory (PTGI) is a tool created by Drs. Richard Tedeschi and Lawrence Calhoun.[3] These men have researched PTG for decades and identified five different categories that signify growth: (1) greater appreciation of life, (2) relationships with others, (3) new possibilities in life, (4) personal strength, and (5) spiritual change. Let's look at each of these categories so you can begin to look for signs of growth within yourself.

- *Greater appreciation of life:* Instead of giving up when things seemed impossible, Joseph found purpose in his daily activities, even in prison. This was recognized by the warden, who put Joseph in charge of the other prisoners.

  Trauma may cause you to look more closely at your own life and your place in the world. As you grow in your appreciation of life, your priorities will likely change. Little things that bring you joy and special moments once taken for granted will become more important. With this greater appreciation for life, you will begin to think more about its purpose and value.

A good sign that you are experiencing growth in this area is a feeling of gratitude. We become more aware of and more thankful for the many little blessings each day brings.

- **Relationships with others:** Instead of giving up on humanity and isolating himself from others, Joseph interacted with his fellow prisoners. He must have developed friendships in prison, because the prisoners trusted him to interpret their dreams. He also developed strong, positive relationships with the warden, and later with the pharaoh.[4]

Although growth will change your relationships with others in positive ways, it doesn't mean all your relationships will improve. You become more discerning as you grow. Some of your relationships will grow in strength and depth while others will be pruned as you start to set confident boundaries. You will find yourself leaning into healthy relationships and distancing yourself from toxicity. You will grow in vulnerability, which is measured as a strength, not a weakness. You will learn to accept that sometimes you need help from others, and you will also desire to be more empathetic when others are struggling. As you begin to feel a sense of belonging, you will begin to cherish people like never before.

- **New possibilities in life:** Instead of resigning himself to a life in prison with no hope of a future, Joseph allowed himself to hope and strive for new possibilities. Before his imprisonment, while serving as a slave, he had been dedicated and true to his master and so was entrusted with great responsibility. In jail, he worked hard to be put into leadership. And then, elevated in a moment from prison to a position of great authority, he served with integrity and wisdom as Pharaoh's second-in-command.

Often we postpone or abandon our dreams out of fear, but those who grow through trauma find that fear no longer holds them back. You might find yourself setting new goals or trying things you wouldn't have thought to try before.

This new perspective can make you more open to taking risks and accepting change. Some people decide to change careers to something they are passionate about or to travel to places they have never been. You may no longer want to continue your same routine because you are ready to live with greater zeal. Excitement about your future is an amazing sign of healing and growth.

- *Personal strength:* Joseph showed incredible personal strength in his ability to overcome adverse circumstances. I imagine that, having survived being thrown into the cistern, he had more confidence he could survive slavery. The longer he survived, the stronger he became in facing hardship.

Those who grow through trauma can look back and see they survived because they were strong. So examine your own situation. You too have survived extremely difficult circumstances. What strengths helped you? If you can identify them, you are headed toward growth. Of course, there will be ups and downs throughout life, but you will become more confident in your ability to handle the tough times. The sweetest by-product of acknowledging your personal strength is optimism.

- *Spiritual change:* Ah! Here is where science points to God. Tedeschi and Calhoun found that those who cope through prayer and learn to rely on God show significant, measurable growth after trauma. Joseph never gave up on God. Instead, he trusted God and became even more aware of how God was caring for him. He used his gifts to serve others and God because he was a man of faith.

Believing in an all-powerful, loving God will help you make sense of life and death. You will be able to focus on finding purpose in living, and you will begin to accept the process of grieving. God's perfect love removes all fear so contentment can take up residence in your soul. Knowing you are not alone on the journey will comfort you in the hard times and always inspire you toward a higher purpose.

We have long believed that adversity can lead to growth. Today some believe the highest levels of growth can't be reached without adversity. This isn't to say everyone needs to experience trauma in order to grow, nor does it mean trauma will always lead to growth. What it tells us is that there is life after trauma, and it can be full of goodness if we take the steps we need in order to heal. Isn't that great news!

When I consider the heroes and prophets in the Bible, I realize God has demonstrated the theory of post-traumatic growth over and over again. Joseph overcame kidnapping, lies, imprisonment, and more. Noah survived the largest flood ever. Job lost everything. Esther was threatened. Moses wandered the wilderness for four decades. Daniel spent the night in a den of hungry lions. Jonah was swallowed by a whale. David battled a giant. Peter lived with shame. Paul was shipwrecked, imprisoned, stoned, and left for dead. Each of these people grew through trauma.

WINTER'S STORY

"Winter" was a young woman who was struggling with severe depression and bipolar disorder when I met her. She had been raised in a Christian home and grew up attending church regularly, but as a young adult she was uncertain what she believed about God. In her desperation, she chased hard after things she thought might bring her happiness. Instead, they led her to some pretty dark places.

Winter began drinking regularly and jumped into several unhealthy relationships, looking for love and physical satisfaction. By age twenty, she was jobless, lacking an education, living with an abusive, controlling man, and pregnant. Although she knew her depression was not getting better in this environment, Winter felt trapped by her own choices. She had come to believe she and her unborn child couldn't survive apart from her boyfriend, whom she depended on for food, shelter, and security.

Winter was an avoider. She was close to her parents at times, but when she knew she was making poor choices, she avoided them. She knew she needed their help, but she didn't want to disappoint them with her circumstances. Instead, in an effort to minimize her situation, she avoided thinking about the abuse, her lack of resources, and her pregnancy. She hadn't even told her parents she was pregnant. By avoiding these topics, Winter was able to pretend everything was just fine . . . until it wasn't.

One night, Winter woke up feeling ill. When she got out of bed, she knew something was wrong. She was weak and dizzy. She convinced her boyfriend to take her to the hospital, where she was told no heartbeat could be found for her baby. She was admitted to the hospital and scheduled for emergency surgery.

If that night hadn't been traumatic enough, the next morning Winter received a call in her hospital room notifying her that the home she shared with her boyfriend had burned to the ground.

Winter lost all her personal belongings, her baby, and finally, her boyfriend. When he learned of the miscarriage, he told Winter he had only been staying with her because of the pregnancy. He was moving out of town and she was on her own.

Lying in her hospital bed, devastated, she wondered whom she could contact and where she might go when she was released. Her parents seemed her only option. She feared telling them about the miscarriage, but she called them. Her parents handled the news with wonderful grace. The comfort they offered their daughter was a perfect picture of unconditional love, and Winter began to remember the lessons she had learned about God's love and mercy.

Winter then asked the most painful question weighing on her heart: "Will I see my baby in heaven someday?"

This tender, vulnerable moment was the first step in Winter's amazing recovery. She opened the door for her parents to pray with her and talk with her about heaven, healing, and hope. Winter moved in with her parents, but only for a short time. Her post-traumatic growth began quickly and progressed beautifully.

Entering therapy, Winter was able to process her trauma, and she received treatment for her underlying mental health issues. It wasn't an easy road for her. She was hospitalized at one point while her medications were adjusted, and she still had to walk through the pain her trauma had caused. But she put one foot in front of the other and persisted in the healing process.

Several years have passed since Winter's trauma, and she has experienced incredible post-traumatic growth. Following her immense loss, Winter has a whole new perspective on and appreciation for life. She realized she didn't need a lot of material things. She discovered that gratitude for simple things brought her great peace.

Her relationships also improved, starting with her and her parents'. Winter began to set boundaries with friends and potential partners. She no longer depended on unhealthy relationships for her sense of security. As she grew stronger in her independence, she realized the future held many possibilities for her. She decided she wanted to help others who struggled like she had. As a result, Winter completed training and became a first responder. Today she is a paramedic and volunteer firefighter.

Not only did Winter find strength she had no idea she possessed, but she now also has a new perspective on God. Her longing to see her child in heaven one day made her curious and caused her to deeply study what the Bible says about the afterlife. Winter now believes it was God who brought her through the storm, and it is God who will carry her forward.

Winter's mental health issues are now successfully managed with medication and therapy. She is married to a man who treats her well, and they have a little girl who brings her great joy. Winter not only survived trauma but grew immensely after it.

FROM BROKEN TO BEAUTIFUL

I have a collection of rocks that reminds me of God's presence in, and watchfulness over, our lives. Some are beautiful gemstones set in silver and gold; others are ugly, rusty rocks. I sometimes ask people to identify which stone is most valuable to them and why. Invariably, people choose one of the cut, set stones. In reality, though, the smallest, ugliest, and rustiest of all the stones is far more valuable than the set ones. You see, that homely little stone is an uncut 37.5-carat ruby. I found it at the top of a mountain, buried deep in the soil. It was difficult to find and difficult to get to. If I hadn't been digging at a known gem mine with the help of someone with a trained eye, I never would have given the rock a second look.

What makes that ugly rock valuable? It has endured extreme pressure over immense periods of time. Buried in the earth, far out of human sight, gemstones are exposed to intense heat and deep-freeze temperatures. What makes the stone valuable is the extreme trauma it endured and the watchful care of God throughout it all.

You are more valuable than any gemstone. God sees you. He doesn't like to see you suffer, but He can use your trauma for His purpose. He has been with you, even when you felt buried and unseen. He has protected you from destruction as you have faced pressure, fire, and hardship. He is the master lapidarist who will refine you into the most beautiful version of yourself possible. Hold on to your hat, because God is creating a new masterpiece in you (Ephesians 2:10). Even now, as He looks into your soul, He is saying, "You are precious!"

Questions for Reflection

1. In what ways do you feel you might be growing—or struggling—in each of the five categories of PTG?

a.   Greater appreciation of life?

b.   Relationships with others?

c.   New possibilities in life?

d.   Personal strength?

e.   Spiritual change?

In his kindness God called you to share in his eternal glory by means of Christ Jesus. So after you have suffered a little while, he will restore, support, and strengthen you, and he will place you on a firm foundation.

1 PETER 5:10 (NLT)

CHAPTER 15

Focusing on Others

Recently I had the opportunity to spend a day at the ocean in South Carolina. I have lived in Michigan most of my life, so oceans are exotic and full of wonder to me. In the morning I woke up very early and went out to walk on the beach. I found myself looking for seashells as I walked. The different colors and patterns captured my interest, and I started to collect those that stood out to me most.

As the morning progressed, more and more people gathered at the beach. I had been walking for an hour or so when I looked around and noticed that every person on the beach had their eyes trained on the seashells that dotted the shore. Some were collecting shells; others, fossils; and still others, shark teeth. It struck me that all these things were remains of creatures that once lived in the ocean. The shoreline was the ocean's wasteland. Every one of these creatures had experienced catastrophic trauma before washing up on the shore, broken and crushed. Yet every person walking on the beach searched the carnage for something beautiful.

I looked out to the ocean. No one seemed to pay attention to that vast beauty, teeming with life beyond anything we can imagine—life that could never survive without that powerful, massive body of water. I stepped into the water and began to wonder about all the life forms that shared the water with me in that moment. Tiny plankton, sharks, crustaceans, whales, fish that could light up the bottom of the ocean . . . creatures my mind can't even fathom.

A verse from Lauren Daigle's song "Love Like This" came to mind, in which the Christian singer calls herself a wasteland given life by God, the living water. I imagined that each wave was God's love washing over me. I walked farther out into the water until the waves were washing up over my shorts. The warm water felt like a gentle massage. I could see waves all the way to the horizon, and I knew they continued far beyond. The waves rolled in perpetually, never slowing their pace, never stopping, consistent, unending.

Isn't this what God's love is like? It washes over us without ceasing. He is the water that brings life to our wasteland. His love is deeper and more vast than any ocean. So why do we fix our eyes on the carnage? While I do believe we can find beauty in brokenness, there comes a time for us to lift our eyes and bear witness to the life that continues all around us.

Following trauma, we tend to focus all our energy on the ruin, don't we? Our pain and grief seem to consume us. We think about our needs, our loss, our anger, our sadness, and the devastation of the trauma. It is natural to focus on self when we stand in the bull's-eye of trauma. As we saw in the ring theory described in chapter 12, it is okay to dump *out* our emotions to others and expect to be comforted *in* . . . at first.

To begin thinking outside ourselves is one of the most difficult things for us to do. Yet it's also one of the most important things when it comes to healing. Studies have shown that remaining in a pattern of self-focus can deepen our pain, lead to a more negative self-image, and keep us stuck in our depression.[1]

One of my favorite Scripture verses says, "He comforts us in all our troubles so that we can comfort others. When they are troubled, we will be able to give them the same comfort God has given us" (2 Corinthians 1:4 NLT). Once we know the comfort of God, we are able to share it with others. As we comfort others, God allows us to find purpose in our own pain.

> *To begin thinking outside ourselves is one of the most difficult yet most important things for us to do when it comes to healing.*

I pray that you are now well into the healing process. If so, it is time to lift your eyes from the wasteland and begin to notice the life that is flourishing around you. As you break the cycle of inward focus, you will begin to notice others who stand in the inner circles of trauma. Now you are in a position to comfort *in*. This shift is how we take our eyes off the wasteland and bear witness to the healing, loving, living water of Jesus. We move from dumping out to comforting in. We begin to comfort others with the comfort we have received.

GETTING STARTED

Start simple, but be intentional in finding ways to focus on others. Just acknowledging that others need compassion can be a powerful first step. Simple acts of kindness, such as smiling at waitstaff or asking a cashier how his or her day is going, can help you pull your focus from self to others. You may even find that the smiles you receive in return brighten your day a bit. These small gestures require little effort but produce great gains.

Make note of the responses you receive. If you journal, you may want to record each daily act of kindness you offered and the response you received. Over time, you may find yourself increasing the time and energy you put into these daily acts. You might even begin to plan them, and you'll begin to look forward to the positive reactions you get. I can almost guarantee you will feel better about yourself and what you have to offer the world.

PRAY FOR OTHERS

Praying for others is an easy but powerful way to share living water. Perhaps you could begin by looking at prayer requests from your church or thinking about friends and family members who need prayer. Create a list and set aside time to pray over those people. You may want to start with just five to fifteen minutes a day.

Once you have your list, let those people know you are praying for them. You can send them a card or a text—or even better, go see them in person. This will physically move you out of your daily routine and place your focus on someone else. Not only will your prayers be a blessing, but your presence could brighten the day for that person—and for you.

SUPPORT GROUPS

Perhaps you have already found help through a support group. A support group is not the same as group therapy. Unlike group therapy, support groups are not led by counselors trained in therapeutic techniques. Instead, members support and learn from one another. Support groups are typically made up of people who have experienced similar traumatic events. These groups reassure us that we are not alone in our pain.

As you know, trauma can be a very lonely place. Often, we don't know anyone else who has experienced what we are living through. But technology has opened doors for online support groups, and these can be invaluable. It is much easier nowadays to find groups that are laser-focused on specific issues. Such a group is also a great way to find information you may be looking for.

You can find a support group for almost anything. I know someone who has been caring for her husband after he was injured in an accident. At one point his heart and breathing stopped for fifteen minutes, but the medical staff were able to resuscitate him. However, as a result of going so long without oxygen, the man now suffers from Lance-Adams syndrome, an extremely rare condition that can occur after successful cardiopulmonary resuscitation.[2] It is so rare that not a single doctor specializes in Lance-Adams in my state of Michigan. But by searching the internet, this woman found an online support group whose members understand exactly what she is dealing with, and through them she has also found other resources to help with treatment.

Joining a support group will bring you not only understanding, acceptance, validation, solidarity, and vital information, but over time the chance to offer support to group members. If you are well into the healing process, imagine what a great resource you could be to others in the group!

While not everyone is called to do so, many trauma survivors find they are able to encourage and console people who experience similar trauma. This is a powerful way to transition from self-focus to helping others, comforting them with the comfort you have received. Remember how lonely you felt in the midst of your trauma? You may be the answer to someone else's loneliness in the journey.

VOLUNTEERING

Volunteering your time to a cause you are passionate about can be rewarding in so many ways. Because volunteers are generally scheduled to serve at specific times, you will be more likely to show up consistently to serve. You can find volunteer activities that involve being around other people, or you can volunteer from your own home.

Start by determining two things: what you are passionate about and what you are good at. If you are passionate about worship and good at music, you could join a praise team. If you are passionate about feeding the hungry and good at cooking, you could volunteer to cook for any number of ministries. For example, some churches cook meals ahead of time and freeze them for when someone is in need; soup kitchens often need cooks and servers; or you could cook for funerals or weddings. If you are passionate about feeding the hungry but are not skilled at cooking, you could help in a food pantry.

You could volunteer at a pregnancy resource center, school, community organization, art gallery, lighthouse, library, Habitat for Humanity, church program, political cause, hospice, museum, historic society, animal shelter, homeless shelter, women's shelter . . . truly, the possibilities are almost endless.

HEROES AND LEGENDS

Serving others can be instrumental in our post-traumatic growth, and we can go on to help others in amazing ways.

Have you ever noticed that heroes and legends all seem to be birthed from a traumatic experience? Clark Kent (Superman) was sent to this planet because his own was destroyed. Peter Parker (Spider-Man) and Bruce Wayne (Batman) were both orphaned when their parents died. Jessica Cruz (Green Lantern) witnessed the murder of several of her friends. Tony Stark (Iron Man) was kidnapped by terrorists. T'Challa's (Black Panther) mother died giving birth to him, and his father was killed when T'Challa was just a young man. Matt Murdock (Daredevil) was blinded as a child when a radioactive substance fell into his eyes after a truck crashed. All these heroes went on to help others who were vulnerable and suffering, but I think we can find more authentic examples in real life.

Joni Eareckson Tada is one such example. She was severely injured in a diving accident at the age of seventeen and has been a quadriplegic ever since. Mrs. Tada could have given up as a teen and succumbed to PTSI, but instead, she grew through her trauma. She became a fierce advocate for the rights of those who suffer from disabilities. She founded the Joni and Friends organization for the purpose of mobilizing Christian churches to minister in disabled communities.

As a result of her work, she was appointed to the National Council on Disability by President Ronald Reagan and later reappointed by President George H. W. Bush. The Americans with Disabilities Act (ADA) was written and signed into law during Mrs. Tada's tenure on this committee. She later served as an advisor to Condoleezza Rice on the Disability Advisory Committee for the US State Department.

Mrs. Tada has written more than fifty books. She has received numerous honorary degrees and awards for her work, including the William Wilberforce Award from the Colson Center on Christian Worldview and the Gold Medallion Lifetime Achievement Award from the Evangelical Christian Publishers Association. She is also known as an artist and radio broadcaster.

I can share much more about the talents and accomplishments of Joni Eareckson Tada, but I am most impressed with her ability to connect with individuals who have suffered traumatic, debilitating injuries. My friend Tracy Michaud is one of those individuals. Tracy was injured as a teen in a terrible car accident, which resulted in her spending over a year in the hospital and having her right leg amputated. Prior to her injury, Tracy had suffered sexual abuse and parental neglect, and the perpetrator of the sexual abuse died in the car accident that took Tracy's leg.

While Tracy was in the hospital, Joni took the time to call her personally. They had a long, encouraging conversation. I asked Tracy what Joni's call meant to her, and this is what she said: "What encouraged me most in talking with Joni was that she understood the lengthy hospitalization, the isolation, and the emotions a teenage girl endures following an accident that causes disability. Although our disabilities are very different, we were able to identify with one another. Even today, the words Joni spoke into my life remain. I struggled for years trying to find my security in other things and people aside from God, but I was encouraged. From that moment on, I knew God was placing that calling in my heart to write a book. Like Joni, I wanted to become an author who would hopefully inspire others."

Tracy Michaud's amazing story of trauma, rebellion, and ultimate redemption can be found in her book, *Broken and Blessed*.[3] She is a normal human being like you and me who was greatly inspired by Joni Eareckson Tada. Joni's words encouraged

Tracy to take the steps to grow through her trauma, and she has experienced the goodness of God in so many ways. Mrs. Tada received comfort from God, which she shared with Tracy, who now is comforting others through her own ministry. It's a beautiful cycle, isn't it?

THE CYCLE OF COMFORT

Those who grow through trauma and then offer comfort to others kick off a cycle that can continue for generations. Tracy may never know how the comfort she has offered might in turn be shared by someone she inspired. But the cycle all begins with accepting the powerful healing of Jesus and then sharing Jesus with others.

> *Those who grow through trauma and then offer comfort to others kick off a cycle that can continue for generations.*

Countless famous heroes from history experienced trauma and then went on to do great things. Maya Angelou experienced child sexual abuse and racism. She went on to be a powerful civil rights activist, poet, writer, dancer, and director. She has inspired millions with her messages of personal strength, resistance, and overcoming adversity.

Helen Keller lost both her sight and hearing before the age of two, likely due to meningitis or scarlet fever. Helen was also unable to speak. As a result of her inability to communicate, many believed she had no hope of growing into a functional adult. Yet she became an educator, humanitarian, and famous author. She was an advocate for disability rights, and her story has inspired generations of people to persist through hardships.

Nelson Mandela was an anti-apartheid activist and lawyer who became a political prisoner in South Africa for standing up for democracy. After spending twenty-seven years in prison, he went on to become the first democratically elected president of South Africa when apartheid finally ended. He has become an icon of democracy and social justice.

Abraham Lincoln's mother died when he was only nine years old, and he battled depression most of his life, yet he went on to become an unforgettable and influential president of the United States. During his time in office, he suffered trauma when his son died of typhoid fever. Somehow, President Lincoln managed to find post-traumatic growth. He led our country through a civil war, issued the Emancipation Proclamation, and influenced the ratification of the Thirteenth Amendment to abolish slavery in the United States.

All these people are famous; their names are well-known. But none of them were born famous. Like you and me, they are mere humans who were children once. They, like us, experienced true pain and suffering before they became the inspirational characters we recognize. None were perfect; they all made mistakes. But they grew through trauma and used their experiences to make a difference for others.

It goes without saying that none of them fixed the world's problems completely, though. There is still much work to be done. Who will carry the torch?

CARRY THE TORCH

Consider some of the people whose stories I have shared in this book.

After healing from the loss of their firstborn son, Dawn and Larry began mentoring other bereaved parents through the grief process. Years later, those same parents returned the comfort when Dawn and Larry's daughter, Melissa, passed away. Out of mutual heartbreak, a beautiful circle of support was born.

Remember Gabrielle, who experienced sexual abuse as a child? She is now a mother herself. She has two children that she is determined to love and protect in ways she never experienced. Besides being an amazing mom, Gabrielle is now completing her studies to become a counselor. She wants to walk with other sexual abuse survivors on the path to healing.

Susan Call survived domestic violence and went on to write and publish her memoir. Many women have contacted Susan to thank her for her encouraging story. She now speaks to women's groups across the nation, sharing a message of strength and empowerment.

One of my personal heroes is my brother, Andy. While he waited for his double lung transplant, he lost his job and his home, but he made sure his family remained intact and strong. It has been nearly two decades since his successful transplant. He still struggles with his health, but he continues his work in engineering and serves in leadership in his church. His children are now grown, married, and serving the Lord in their own ways. Andy and his wife, Kristie, demonstrate what a strong marriage looks like as they continue their incredible love story. Andy has encouraged many people facing transplant surgery. Some have lived, some have not, but he made sure that each of them heard about Jesus and knew about both healing and heaven. He traveled to one patient's hometown to baptize her prior to her transplant surgery. I know Andy will be dancing in heaven one day with those he introduced to the comfort of knowing Jesus. For now, he is a living example of love and inspiration.

I am happy to say God has provided ministry opportunities for me as well. At the time I was attacked in college, I had every intention of completing my degree in music. I was passionate about music and wanted to teach young students to love it as much as I did. I couldn't have imagined a career doing anything else. But not long after my trauma, I changed my major to political science. I wanted to study law in grad school and become a prosecuting attorney so I could put masked men behind bars.

Upon graduating, I applied to law school and began working a clerkship with a large legal firm in northern Ohio. Only a few months into this position, I discovered with horror that only about 0.5 percent of rapists were convicted and sent to prison. (Today that number has increased, but only to a dismal 2.5 percent.) As long as perpetrators of this violent crime were not being prosecuted, I knew that victims would need counseling. So I immediately changed my grad school plans and studied counseling and college-student personnel instead of law. At the time, I thought college students would be the population I served, but God had other plans. Today I counsel in private practice and help people of all ages recover from trauma.

I had been counseling for decades when I received word that my attacker had been identified. It is no coincidence that this occurred only days after I told God I was giving my story to Him and letting go of it myself. As I've said, I truly thought I knew enough by that time to be immune from PTSI, but this wasn't the case. Facing my own battle for healing has made me a better, more sensitive and insightful counselor. God uses everything, doesn't He?

God began to open doors I never could have predicted. Besides writing, I speak regularly. I have met many survivors of sexual violence in my travels and have been able to offer the comfort I received from Jesus while on my healing journey. What an honor it is to share about His healing power! But God didn't stop there. He opened doors for me to address legislators in Lansing, Michigan, and Washington, DC, and He has used my story to influence legislation that could lead to protection and justice for many in this country. I don't know yet where my efforts will lead, but I remember all God has accomplished so far. He will use my story for His purpose, even if I don't know what that may look like.

Friend, you never know how God plans to use you and your story. Will you carry the torch of comfort to others to be prepared for how he does use you? Depending on where you are in the healing process, you may or may not feel ready. If not, that's okay. Give yourself time. Continue to take steps toward healing and post-traumatic growth. Give your pain to Jesus today and ask Him to do with it as He sees fit. Perhaps He will bury it in the expansive ocean of His love. Or maybe He plans to put you in a position to make a difference in someone else's life. None of us can guess how God will use our story—but we can trust that He *will* use it if we let Him.

Questions for Reflection

1. Has anyone comforted you after having survived their own trauma experience? Who?

2. Have you reached a point in your healing process where you think about supporting others? If so, what ideas have you been thinking about?

The man who gives much will have much,
and he who helps others will be helped himself.

PROVERBS 11:25 (NLV)

CHAPTER 16

And a Partridge in a Pear Tree

---

*I*f you live in a country that celebrates Christmas, my guess is a tune popped into your mind as soon as you read this chapter's title. "A partridge in a pear tree" is the first gift mentioned in the Christmas carol "The Twelve Days of Christmas." The verses are rich in Christian symbolism. While you may find several interpretations of the various gifts, the partridge is commonly understood to represent Jesus. That's because a mother partridge is willing to die to save her young, just as Jesus willingly died to save us.

But what does the pear tree represent? I found several different interpretations, but the one I love is that the pear tree represents you and me. That means the partridge in the pear tree is Christ in us. As the song progresses, its verses become longer, but each returns to the partridge in the pear tree, and thus the same point: Christ in us.

In chapter 11 we talked about the importance of remaining connected to the Vine. Remember? Jesus tells us to abide, or persist, in Him, *as He abides in us* (John 15:4). God initiates that relationship by persistently pursuing us; He wants us to be equally persistent in following Him.

Throughout this book I have told the story of my New Bradford Pear tree. It is a true story, and I love that it just happened to involve a pear tree. If you haven't guessed by now, the tree in my story doesn't just represent me. It also represents you. I know you have experienced a crushing blow like my tree did. You have been wounded, and it will take time to heal. I also know you have been created with all you need to survive, heal, and grow. You too were born with certain strong characteristics (taproots). You have a root system that can access all you need for survival and beyond. These are the things that will help you to stay *in Christ*, just as He is *in you*.

If you're still not sure what it means to have Christ in you, let me take a moment to explain. God came to the earth in the form of Jesus, and when Jesus left this world, the Holy Spirit remained to live in us.

Before Jesus, the only way people could make up for their sins was to make a sacrifice to God. The greatest sacrifice was an unblemished, prized lamb. Jesus is often referred to as the Lamb of God. He was perfect in every way because He is God— God in human flesh. When Jesus died on the cross, He became the ultimate sacrifice. Jesus suffered the shame, pain, and agony of the cross, and God suffered the loss of His child for one reason alone: so you and I could be forgiven of our sins. That is powerful love, isn't it—for Jesus, the Lamb of God, to willingly lay down His life for us, even knowing we would sin in the future?

Before He died, Jesus assured His people that He would give us the Holy Spirit to comfort and guide. The only requirement for the Holy Spirit to live in us is that we believe Jesus is God and that He died for our sins. My friend, if you believe Jesus is who He says He is and you believe He did what the Bible said He did, the Holy Spirit is already living within you.

This is great news because it means you are never alone. The God of the universe is breathing His goodness into your life, comforting your soul and healing your pain. When you are in the lowest valley, He is right there with you. He knows everything you are facing, feeling, and fearing. He has the power, mercy, and grace to meet your needs whenever you call on Him. He loves you when you are at your best, and He loves you when you are at your worst. Once you decide to let Him live in your pear tree, there is nothing you can do that would make Him move out.

> *You are never alone. The God of the universe is breathing His goodness into your life, comforting your soul and healing your pain.*

I know some of you may be struggling with God right now. Perhaps you are mad at God, or wondering why He didn't prevent your trauma from occurring. It is normal to have these feelings, and to question why. I hope you are sharing your thoughts with Him and allowing Him to respond. The R.A.W. journaling tips (chapter 9) are a great way to start that conversation. In the meantime, let's look at what we know about God.

TRUTHS ABOUT GOD

The events we experience in the land of the living may never make sense to us. God's perspective is from a much higher point of view. We can't possibly see the whole picture the way He does. The key is trust—trust that God knows the entire picture, and that He knows what is needed for you to walk through this storm. When we consider what we know about God's character, it becomes easier for us to trust Him. Let's take a look at truths the Bible tells us about God.

> Trust in the LORD with all your heart;
> do not depend on your own understanding.
>
> Seek his will in all you do,
> and he will show you which path to take.
> (Proverbs 3:5–6 NLT)

We know God loves us with a love so extravagant we can't possibly understand it. His love is unconditional and never fails us. There is nothing you can do that would make Him stop loving you.

> I am convinced that neither death nor life, neither angels nor demons, neither the present nor the future, nor any powers, neither height nor depth, nor anything else in all creation, will be able to separate us from the love of God that is in Christ Jesus our Lord. (Romans 8:38–39)

We know God is not vindictive or wicked. He doesn't cause our trauma as punishment for anything we have done wrong. We learned about this in the book of Job, but we are reassured that God isn't wicked throughout Scripture.

> He will not constantly accuse us,
>   nor remain angry forever.
> He does not punish us for all our sins;
>   he does not deal harshly with us, as we deserve.
>   (Psalm 103:9–10 NLT)

While God doesn't purpose for us to experience trauma, He can use all things for His purposes. Humans were given the freedom to make their own choices, good and bad. Sometimes these choices lead to trauma. God is grieved over this, but He keeps His promise that we are free to choose. Our free will is why Jesus told us we would experience trouble in the land of the living.

But even when trouble comes, God can use it for good.

> We know that in all things God works for the good of those who love him, who have been called according to his purpose. (Romans 8:28)

We will never be alone in our pain and suffering. Even when it feels like God is absent, He will be right beside you. He will never leave you to suffer alone.

> Be strong and courageous. Do not be afraid or terrified be-
> cause of them, for the LORD your God goes with you; he will
> never leave you nor forsake you. (Deuteronomy 31:6)

Be encouraged by the character traits of God, who wants to take up residence in your heart. He is trustworthy and compassionate. I pray that you will give Him a chance to show you His love and mercy.

MADE NEW

Had my tree been the original Bradford Pear variety (*Pyrus calleryana* "Brad-ford"), I believe it never would have survived the crushing blow of the larger pine. But my New Bradford Pear (*P. calleryana* "Holmford") had been cultivated differently. This tree had a stronger trunk and superior branch distribution. It wasn't prone to breaking or splitting during mild windstorms. Though the New Bradford Pear maintains the positive qualities of the original Bradford Pear—both trees have beautiful white flowers in the spring and display vibrant colors in the fall—it is stronger than the original Bradford Pear. The trunk of my New Bradford Pear has grown straight and true, and its branches are balanced. The New Bradford Pear was created with all it needed to survive the storms it would encounter. The difference between the trees? The *New* Bradford tree had been made new.

When we are *in Christ*, we too are made new. Second Corinthians 5:17 says, "If anyone is in Christ, the new creation has come: The old has gone, the new is here!" You have been made new by the Master Gardener, the one who knows exactly what you need to be resilient. I can't imagine anything that could bring us more peace of mind than to know that the God of the universe is working on us and making a new creation.

I love these words from the book of Isaiah:

> Forget the former things;
>   do not dwell on the past.
> See, I am doing a new thing!
>   Now it springs up; do you not perceive it?
> I am making a way in the wilderness
>   and streams in the wasteland.
>   (Isaiah 43:18–19)

There is so much packed into these two verses. Though we will not forget our trauma nor get *over* it, we will get *through* it. Stay focused on the future with hope, because God is doing something new. He is planning to bring joy into your life once again. He is making a way for you to get *through* tough times, just like he parted the Red Sea to help others who were struggling. God has no intention of leaving you in the wasteland; He is washing over you with his love, refreshing and restoring your soul.

If a gardener can make the Bradford Pear into a new creation, imagine what God can do with you. He gives every resource you need to walk this journey. We are redeemed by the power of the Holy Spirit who lives within us.

The joy of being made new is the promise of a fresh start and redemption from our pain. What does it mean to redeem? When searching for synonyms and related words, I found many: *save, reclaim, recover, deliver, rescue, restore, satisfy, rehabilitate, regenerate, restore, repair,* and *renew.*

That little word, *redeem,* is a powerful word, isn't it?

Remember, we are made new when we are *in Christ.* I want *you* to know the living water that brings healing. That water can be found only in Jesus, and the more you drink of that living water, the more sustaining it will be.

May the same sunshine of hope that shone on my tree shine on you as well. Soak it in, friend. Take the steps that lead to the healing He wants to pour over you. May you blossom again and find the goodness of the Lord in the land of the living.

I pray these things for you: strong taproots, a deep root system, mended wounds, hope, strength of spirit, persistence, confidence, a sense of purpose, compassion for others, and most importantly . . . a partridge in a pear tree.

The Partridge in *your* pear tree.

Questions for Reflection

1. What are your honest feelings toward God today? Share these feelings with Him.

2. In what ways do you see, or hope to see, the goodness of the Lord today?

I remain confident of this: I will see the goodness of the LORD in the land of the living.

PSALM 27:13

Acknowledgments

All praise and glory to Jesus, without whom I would have no basis for sharing the comfort I have received. His mercy has no limits.

Thank you to my husband. I watched you cook our meals, build our home, attend to our grandchildren, and take care of the dog for many weeks while I worked on this book. You have been my cheerleader, sounding board, common-sense coordinator, and comic relief. Your support means the world to me.

My children and grandchildren, you embody the goodness of the Lord in the land of the living. I love you all to the moon.

I want to express my deep gratitude to all who have prayed over this book and all who will read it. I am so grateful for Cynthia Ruchti: agent extraordinaire, encourager, prayer warrior, and sage adviser. I can't count the number of times I have thanked the Lord for you. I am also grateful for my first editor, Andy Rogers. You have the gift of encouragement, my friend. I learned so much from you in this process.

Thank you to my dear friend Angeline Boulley. I am so proud of you and all you have achieved. I can't think of anyone else I would have rather had write the foreword to this book. You have been a friend for life, an inspiration, and a delight. I can't wait to see all that the Lord does in your life.

So many friends deserve to be acknowledged here. Thank you to all who have prayed me through this process and who have offered encouraging words. Susan Call, the queen of metaphors and similes—your support has been as faithful as the sunrise, your guidance as steady as a metronome, and your friendship as precious as rubies. Thank you for keeping me focused and holding me accountable.

Shaunna, Dawn, Linda, and Mychelle have literally been on this journey with me. Thank you for traveling with me as I speak in places far and wide. Many have seen you working at my back table, but most have no idea that you are the prayer warriors behind the scenes. You minister to those who share their own trauma stories following these events. I will forever cherish our talk time from our travels together.

Thank you to all who allowed me to share their precious, sacred stories. You are the finest examples of healing grace. Your strength and faithfulness have moved me to the core, and I know your stories will bless many with hope.

My gratitude runs deep for Rachel, Catherine, and the rest of the Kregel Publications team. You have been kinder to me than I knew a publishing house could be.

Finally, thank you to my dear friend Deb. Your faith in the face of trauma never wavered. You taught me how to trust in God regardless of the circumstances that surround me. I miss your smile and your creative genius. I can't wait to sing together again one day. I will see you in heaven, dear friend.

Notes

Foreword

1. André B. Rosay, "Violence Against American Indian and Alaska Native Women and Men," *NIJ Journal* 277 (September 2016): 38–45, https://nij.ojp.gov/topics/articles/violence-against-american-indian-and-alaska-native-women-and-men.

Introduction

1. Oxford Advanced Learner's Dictionary, "victim," accessed March 24, 2024, https://www.oxfordlearnersdictionaries.com/us/definition/english/victim.

The Parable of the Pear Tree

1. The metaphor of a pear tree isn't meant to minimize pain in any way. But you may find—as I and many of my clients have—that what happened to the tree in its most traumatic moment and after is a story that allows us to look deeply into trauma while maintaining a buffer between the pain and our humanity. When survival seems unattainable, I hope the parable of the tree will help us navigate the most difficult topics.

Chapter 6: Avoiding Artificial Coping

1. Katherine L. Mills et al., "Trauma, PTSD, and Substance Use Disorders: Findings from the Australian National Survey of Mental Health and Well-Being," *American Journal of Psychiatry* 163, no. 4 (2006): 652–58, https://doi.org/10.1176/ajp.2006.163.4.652; Martina Reynolds et al., "Co-Morbid Post-Traumatic Stress Disorder in a Substance Misusing Clinical Population," *Drug and Alcohol Dependence* 77, no. 3 (2005): 251–58, https://doi.org/10.1016/j.drugalcdep.2004.08.017.

Chapter 7: Managing the Unmanageable

1. Dictionary.com, "prune," accessed September 19, 2024, https://www.dictionary.com/browse/prune.

2. Henry Cloud and John Townsend, *Boundaries: When to Say Yes, How to Say No to Take Control of Your Life*, updated ed. (Zondervan, 2017).

Chapter 8: Mending the Wounds

1. Frank Ochberg, "An Injury, Not a Disorder," Dart Center for Journalism and Trauma, September 19, 2012, https://dartcenter.org/content/injury-not-disorder-0.

2. Bessel van der Kolk, *The Body Keeps the Score: Brain, Mind, and Body in the Healing of Trauma* (Penguin, 2015).

Chapter 9: Cultivating the Healing Process at Home

1. For more information on writing R.A.W., or to purchase a black-paged Bright Future Journal, go to www.LisaSaruga.com. Proceeds from the

sales of these journals help fund my legislative efforts to write a brighter future for survivors of sexual violence.

2. "About Us," Music for the Soul, accessed August 1, 2024, https://www.musicforthesoul.org/about-music-for-the-soul.

Chapter 10: Finding Hope

1. Dictionary.com, "hope," accessed September 19, 2024, https://www.dictionary.com/browse/hope.

Chapter 11: Harnessing the Power of Persistence

1. Susan Call, *A Search for Purple Cows: A True Story of Hope* (Guideposts Books, 2013).

Chapter 12: When People Say the Wrong Thing

1. Susan Silk and Barry Goldman, "How Not to Say the Wrong Thing," *Los Angeles Times*, April 7, 2013, https://www.latimes.com/nation/la-oe-04 07-silk-ring-theory-20130407-story.html.

2. This is why I recommend reading the book of Job *later* in your healing process. Job's resolution is Job's story; to assume that your story will be the same would harm rather than help.

Chapter 13: Guilt and Shame

1. Brené Brown, *I Thought It Was Just Me (but It Isn't): Making the Journey from "What Will People Think?" to "I Am Enough"* (Avery, 2007), 197.

Chapter 14: Post-Traumatic Growth

1. Richard G. Tedeschi and Lawrence G. Calhoun, "The Posttraumatic Growth Inventory: Measuring the Positive Legacy of Trauma," *Journal of Traumatic Stress* 9, no. 3 (1996): 468, https://doi.org/10.1002/jts.2490090305.

2. You can read all of Joseph's story in Genesis 37–50.

3. Tedeschi and Calhoun, "Posttraumatic Growth Inventory," 455–71.

4. Genesis 40 and 41.

Chapter 15: Focusing on Others

1. See, for instance, Tom Pyszczynski and Jeff Greenberg, "Self-Regulatory Perseveration and the Depressive Self-Focusing Style: A Self-Awareness Theory of Reactive Depression," *Psychological Bulletin* 102, no. 1 (1987): 122–38, https://doi.org/10.1037/0033-2909.102.1.122.

2. Ha Lim Lee and Ju Kang Lee, "Lance-Adams Syndrome," *Annals of Rehabilitation Medicine* 35, no. 6 (2011): 939, https://doi.org/10.5535/arm.2011.35.6.939.

3. Tracy Michaud, *Broken and Blessed: How God Set Me Free from Abuse, Dysfunctional Relationships, and Generational Sin* (Redemption Press, 2022).

ABOUT THE AUTHOR

Lisa Saruga

Lisa Saruga is a licensed professional counselor, EMDR trauma therapist, speaker, and author. She's certified as a legal and ethical specialist by the American School Counselor Association. Her advocacy extends to her legislative efforts for survivor justice and her impactful contributions as a writer, notably in Carolyn B. Stone's *School Counseling Principles: Ethics and Law*. Her debut book, *The Trauma Tree*, signifies a new chapter in her commitment to empowering others. Find her at LisaSaruga.com.